PRAYER AT THE HEART OF LIFE

Prayer
at the Heart of Life

Pierre-Yves Emery

Translated by
William J. Nottingham

ORBIS BOOKS
MARYKNOLL, NEW YORK

Originally published as *La Prière au coeur de la vie*
by Les Presses de Taizé, 1971.

Copyright © 1975, Orbis Books,
Maryknoll, New York 10545

Library of Congress Catalog Card Number 74-17870

ISBN: 0-88344-393-7

Manufactured in the United States of America

CONTENTS

Foreword

This is not just a book about prayer. It is a book of realistic theology. It grew out of discussions between a brother of the Taizé Community and young couples in France who were not afraid to face the most serious contradictions in trying to live as Christians today. In dealing with prayer, they were basically wrestling with other questions about the existence of God and the chances of human fulfillment, under the political and psychological conditions of their generation. The result is a theological undergirding that is missing in much devotional literature and a disclosure of the magnificence of God that is missing in many works of Christian social ethics.

There are plenty of books to reinforce American piety and to encourage the individualistic faith experience of these charismatic and spiritualistic times. But this one takes the modern world seriously—the whole world, at that, with the sufferings and hopes of millions. It recognizes the importance of the religious community—celibate or familial—in helping people to find communion with God, through meaningful worship on one hand and solidarity with the oppressed on the other. Prayer is "where the action is" at the heart of life, a metaphysical as well as a social supposition, but the worldwide Church of Jesus Christ gives concreteness to the message and experience from which prayer originates in the individual person. Unlike much popular religious writing, the accent here is not on personal subjectivity alone, but on the work of God both in the extended family of his Church—gathered and dispersed—and in the intercontinental ferment where his compassion is mirrored in every struggle for justice.

As with the "individual," so with the "universal." Prayer among the peoples of other ancient religions, the spirituality of various forms of "new" religions, and the non-prayer of atheistic or ideological movements deserve respect and the expression of fraternal love, but they are not the same as Christian prayer, which is "in Christ." The Church, by which is meant the truly ecumenical or catholic tradition among the churches, tends toward a specific historical humanism through the Gospel which is preached, the Bible which is read, the Bread which is broken, the baptism which is sealed in the name of the Father, Son, and Holy Spirit. Christian prayer cannot be abstracted from the Christian Church, as the citations in this book from the saints and martyrs, past and present, so clearly intimate. The Trinity remains as a frame of reference for any theological innovation, and the incarnation makes human solidarity in sorrow and joy inescapably real.

The book speaks for itself: an affirmation that prayer is necessary for most of us and has its place in a new sociopolitical context. The author is a member of the Taizé Community in central France, bringing to his practical analysis of prayer an ecumenical background particularly rich for Protestants, Catholics, and Orthodox alike. It is said that the first audience that Pope John XXIII granted was to representatives of Taizé! Since 1940, the Community has grown to about 100 and has exercised an ever-widening range of influence for *Christian unity* and for *Christian presence* among the poor, from staff positions at the World Council of Churches in Geneva, Switzerland, to fraternities of laborers or students in Marseille, Chicago, Abidjian, Recife, and elsewhere. They have been prolific in publications, including an ecumenical version of the New Testament in Spanish, made available as a gift to Catholic and Pentecostal congregations in Spain and Latin America. Some members of the community have served as pastors of Lutheran churches in France; others have been team workers of CIMADE, the French ecumenical service agency. On August 30, 1974, a long-awaited international Council of Youth took place at Taizé, a reported 30,000 young people attending the first of a series of events expected to take place throughout the world. Prior Roger Schutz has written: "We have made ourselves listen to the young people from five continents. We have learned that among a very large number of them there is a thirst for God, but at the same time the will to move forward in the service of man. For them, it is all or nothing. When they understand Christ, it is above all a *life*. When they understand the Church, they want it to be *creative*."

Crossing confessional lines in authentic and discerning inclusiveness as a contemporary monk of Swiss Protestant origins, Brother Pierre-Yves speaks a language that is at the same time familiar and strangely new to most American Christians. The fact that the book is written by a Protestant monk in France gives a special dimension to the Church and to faith. France has experienced deep tensions between modern secular philosophies, which makes it impossible to take either the gospel or Marxism for granted. Nowhere is there such a development of technological elitism as in the new city called "Paris 2000 A.D." or the futuristic Charles de Gaulle Airport, with their long-range commitments for a style of life and economic power. Struggles against Third World exploitation by multinational corporations are clearly drawn by intellectuals, the labor movement, leftists, and liberals. Socialism is a live option in political elections. Since the "revolution" of May 1968, there have been radical demands and programs for popular participation in structural change of institutions and industries, with a corresponding repression of groups or actions that have been too threatening. Churches have become divided. Theologians interpreting the social reality of France and Europe have made political and ideological commitments that have caused scandal, soul-searching, and the pursuit of new directions. For these reasons, the book has a special vigor and freshness for Americans, not because it is revolutionary, but because it faces all the revolutionary criticisms and the "crisis of faith" of many modern Christians.

There are three special reasons why *Prayer at the*

Heart of Life brings valuable perspective to the American situation:

1. *Concerning the Bible.* A new concern for prayer or religious experience does not need to be a blind acceptance of biblical literalism. Nor can it continue very long knowing little of the content and background of the Bible. This book is based on a culturally intelligent reading of Scripture, poles apart from the facile fundamentalism of American culture religion and much of the current religious revival. Yet it generates loving respect and insight toward the Bible in the discovery and deepening of faith. Emery has previously written books of biblical research. Christian prayer cannot be separated from Scripture, and Scripture cannot be separated from historical and textual scholarship. This must not lead to professorial isolation but rather to an attitude of objectivity, an inquiring and open mind, an appreciation of the grace of God in the uniqueness of Jewish history, and at least a partial awareness of the concreteness and complexity of ancient times.

This book argues for a renewal of prayer and inner communion among Christians, while regarding the Bible in a mature and critical way. The rediscovery of piety does not require us to make the Bible a book of magic or end-of-the-world forecasts. Nor does it call for twentieth-century cultural schizophrenia by absorbing Hellenistic belief in spirits and demons, common in the New Testament. Prayer calls for the study of and meditation on the Bible at different levels, but never as a literal and uniform revelation "cover to cover," unaffected by intricate historical and contextual conditioning. On the contrary, the early forms of ancient Middle Eastern culture, language, and political imperialism provide the vehicle by which the People was born and through them the Book and the Christ. Their liberation from slavery in Egypt by God who "saw their affliction and heard their cry" and then required mercy toward the widow, the orphan, and the alien, is essential to the understanding of why and to whom prayer is made.

2. *Technology and Social Realism.* The rediscovery of our need for prayer, which technology itself sees in emotional and psychological terms, is not necessarily alienating in the modern world. On the contrary, it can be liberating and humanizing. It can be a way in which creative human values survive and protest against oppressive systems. It can keep a person strong under the pressures of repressive ideologies or the violence and power of one class, race, or nation over another. Rubem Alves, Protestant theologian and author of *Tomorrow's Child* (Harper and Row), has been pointing in this direction in his recent articles in Brazil.

In this book, the continuing scientific process and increasingly technological organization of life are not rejected. The calendar cannot be reversed. The search and research for truth must be followed wherever it leads. Therefore, a new vigor in Jewish–Christian religious practice is not considered to require an absence from the process but rather a creative participation at some points, a critical resistance at others. The nature of the universe and the knowledge of man are seen in their most recently delineated features, not blithely ignored in favor of spiritualist imaginings and neosupernaturalism. It seems as if there are cracks appearing in our intellectual framework, and a movie like *The Exorcist* brings out the latent superstition of a metaphysically impoverished culture. But the piety of faith is not irrational. It strengthens the very fabric of reason, because it is based on trust.

Religious infantilism and secularism often go together. A Broadway play called *Jumpers* toys with the idea that at some time or other in human history "the onus of proof passed from the atheist to the believer." The assumption that "God is" fell into widespread disuse as the ultimate reference for the meaning of existence and moral values, when "quite suddenly and secretly the *noes* had it." The further implausibility of believing in God in a technological age is aptly put by the playwright, Tom Stoppard: "While a man might believe that the providence of sheep's wool was made in heaven, he finds it harder to believe the same of dacron polyester!"

No wonder prayer becomes a rarity! No wonder the particular wisdom and serenity associated with prayer become lost arts even to people of the churches! The question is not whether belief in God is supported by "common sense" today, but what a sense of communion with God can mean for personal courage and hope. What can it mean for the unceasing effort to devise just social institutions? How can it fail to help us cut through social ideologies that justify intolerable indifference to human rights and institutionalized violence?

Prayer is not portrayed here as an alluring alienation from the bitter reality of hazard, loneliness, and death—or of racism, economic exploitation, and the ideological manipulation of technological power. It is no withdrawal for the sake of a false security. A scientific worldview, however intense, and technological capacity, however vast, simply present different prospects when viewed from the needs of the world's poor and from the criterion of faith in the God who is known to us because he delivers the *oppressed*. But it is from within that cultural combination rather than from without that the Christian will find his or her vocation and the sense of Christian community. And this book shows why secularism alone, like spiritualism, does not satisfy the deepest intellectual craving of many of us.

3. *Solidarity with the Third World.* If prayer is at the heart of life, it finds there the appalling provincialism of a great many American Christians. Our newspapers are especially lacking in news from the continents of Africa, Asia, Latin America, and other regions. Television brings even less, with more advertising! News from the rest of the world is of interest, according to the observation of a student from Jamaica, only when it is irresistibly sensational or tied to the national interest of our own country. Although not specific, this book shows an awareness of the great issues facing the world, to which the daily work and presence of Christians are inexorably linked. It is necessary to hear the developing nations' cry for international economic justice, if the American renewal of prayer and religious life is not going to be just another form of selfishness.

Relating to the peoples of the long-exploited regions, the former colonies, the areas once known as "the mission field" are not often emphasized by the new evangelism, inside or outside the churches, even though the rich nations have become dependent on these countries for natural resources, raw materials, and cheap labor. The Jesus movement and the Christian Businessmen's groups never heard of UNCTAD, torture in Brazil, or tiger cages. When even the missionaries start providing information about neocolonialism, U.S. supported dictatorships, multinational corporation piracy, and the consumer imperialism of the middle class around the world, it is considered by some a breach of ministerial ethics. Reports on Chile or Korea are supposed to be about "church growth" and soul-winning, not ITT and the CIA. Americans tend to be moved to pity for the poor but not to political awareness and action for and with them.

At the heart of life in America is the ambiguity of being economically and militarily related to the whole world and personally awakened only to limited parts of it, usually along racial lines. But prayer points to a universality which is not encompassed by personal experience or ethnic affinity. This is what is overlooked by those who accuse the "activists" of the 1960's of neglecting spiritual concerns. The "action" came from the spiritual concern, and many of America's foremost religious leaders did their praying in the face of public rejection and sometimes in jail. The current return to personal piety must not be allowed to hide the wounds of the world and serve as an excuse for the general ineffectiveness of local churches. The love of God is the source of personal salvation because it is known by faith to be infinite and suffering love for human beings everywhere. And today, two out of three of those human beings do not have enough to eat.

Dom Helder Camara, archbishop of Recife-Olinda, Brazil, upon receiving an honorary doctor of laws degree from Harvard University, June 13, 1974, for his defense of human rights and philosophy of nonviolent social change, said: "Why do we still wait to recognize officially *misery* as the bloodiest of wars, when statistics prove that misery deforms and kills more people than nuclear or biochemical war?" In the 1970 Orbis Books biography of Dom Helder, entitled *The Violence of a Peacemaker*, he is called a "Third World Spokesman," calling to the attention of all Christians the fact that during the United Nations Decade of Development the gap between rich and poor nations widened. During the period that the United States invested in Latin America 13.7 billion dollars, its earnings amounted to 23.2 billion, a suction of capital from overseas of 9.5 billion dollars. The problem is simply that the poor nations help to make the rich nations richer. This is why investment advertisements in *Newsweek* read, "Money grows faster in Mexico." It is why trade commissions from Indiana go to Brazil and assembly factories are being built in Haiti by American companies.

This recognition of solidarity with the Third World, where two-thirds of the earth's population lives, is important in any lay witness or evangelistic endeavor. To become sensitive to the domination in which Third World countries are held by the great powers and by their own Herod-like governing classes is a central part of what well-to-do Western Christians can do for their own souls. The concern for the struggles, hunger, labor, creativity, and freedom of these countries makes an attitude of prayer something more than private religion. It is obedience to the mystical criterion of the cross of Jesus Christ, with its hope of resurrection.

*   *   *   *   *

Seldom does the "theology of liberation" deal with worship. Seldom does pastoral theology deal with social ethics. But this dichotomy is as false as it is unnecessary. It is probably even unintentional! We need to find God at the heart of life in a new and revivifying way. We need to see theology as critical reflection on what is *done*, in the light of faith, so that history is transformed for the liberation of men and women. Theology is not just elaboration of confessional traditions. But the reflection is more than social analysis. It is also participation in the reality of God, through which his grace creates a new dynamic of love and justice in the world.

Faith is not theology; it is the precondition of theology. According to Jesus, the first and greatest commandment is not to believe in God but *to love him*, with all your heart, soul, mind, and strength (Mark 12:30; Deut. 6:5). And while theology must arise out of *praxis*, or actual involvement in the making and changing of history and culture, it is God known in faith and prayer who is the reason for any theology at all.

Margaret Mead said not long ago, "The thing the churches must do is address themselves to the religious question." This means the mystery of God. But according to the biblical and liturgical traditions of the Christian Church, God makes peace, justice, health, and hunger "religious questions." This book by Frère Pierre-Yves puts the emphasis where it belongs, with a classical competence that Americans will find thoughtful and enriching. *God himself is the Liberator.* That is why the authentic religion of Jesus is integral human liberation. And in this book about God there is a breadth of spirit concerning the Bible, technology and social realism, and solidarity with the Third World, which is the only basis on which the American churches can attain credibility among their young people and be true to their own confession of faith. The recovery of prayer is not in itself the hope of the world, but as response to God, who is uniting people in the struggle to affirm and dignify life for *all* peoples, it is indispensable. Prayer is not the only way to know his love nor the only means of unrelentingly resisting evil and death, but for many it is a necessary recourse of the human mind and heart. Above all, it is a triumph of grace.

We need to bring into the liberation process a heightened awareness not only of our disastrous bondage to the social structure and to sin, but also of our own freedom in the communion God gives in his Spirit. For this, the pages that follow might be a source of new perceptions. They are certainly an invitation to a deeper commitment to the God who has reconciled the world unto himself and redeemed it for the joy and peace of all.

William J. Nottingham

Preface

This is not a scholarly book. It does not aspire to be either systematic or comprehensive. The subject of prayer is so vast and has been dealt with so often that one can permit himself to roam about rather freely, emphasizing one point, passing hurriedly over another, and being silent on a third.

The book begins with a question many Christians are asking today: how can we pray under the conditions of present-day life? But behind "how" lies another question: does prayer still have any meaning in the modern world; is it worth the trouble of discussing it? It is useless even to wish to deal with "how" before paying attention to "why."

Therefore, one discovers still a third question, on which the question of prayer closely depends: what relationship is there between God and modern men, who spend their daily lives in a technological society, in the midst of rapid and chaotic world change?

Because of these questions, this book begins with a chapter on the theme of God and man's world. If prayer is not to seem marginal to our human action, to our work, to our commitments, to our leisure, it is first essential that God not seem marginal to human life itself or to the world in which life is spent.

Then, in the second chapter we will be better able to see how prayer and human action have a very necessary and profound relationship. This reciprocal relationship can be described as: prayer, the heart of human action; and action, the body of prayer.

Deliberately avoiding any attempt to provide a recipe, the third chapter approaches prayer, not in its outward forms, but within its inner movement, which is here called "contemplation."* There is, in fact, no point in hurrying to the most pressing, the most facile, the most external, or the most "practical" questions. One may think himself concrete when he is only being superficial. Like all important things, prayer is exacting, even when one merely reflects on it. Accepting that fact is my way of being concrete. The third chapter, therefore, tries to clarify, at least in part, some topics which are problems today: the feeling of God's absence, the language of faith and of prayer, the awareness of man's need for God, and the role of emotions in that awareness.

The difficulties with prayer today revolve around the particular forms that prayer requires. So the fourth chapter discusses these issues, especially asking what happens to intercession in a civilization that seeks to solve all man's problems and suffering through science and technology. Are we forced to oscillate endlessly (or make a choice) between a

*The author uses *oraison* to indicate the deeply personal devotion that underlies the act of prayer itself. Precise translation is difficult; "contemplation" has been used throughout this text. Other synonyms are "communion" or "silent prayer" [Translator's Note].

naiveté which is limited to superstition and a positivism which eliminates faith?

Finally, the last two chapters deal with more specific subjects: liturgical prayer in the midst of the tensions that are arising in its current renewal; and the meaning of the prayer of married couples and some of its special difficulties.

* * * * *

These pages include many quotations, often from authors of past centuries. There is nothing wrong in recalling that others have preceded us and that we have not invented everything, not even our problems. Additionally, nothing is lost in pointing out how certain things from the past retain their freshness. However, the purpose here is not historical, and the choice of quotations is subjective and not at all systematic. The quotations play the role that illustrations often have in a book, providing rest and joy for the spirit. They are also included to emphasize the character I have sought to give to this work—that of a meditation, already close to prayer itself.

* * * * *

The thoughts developed in this book owe much to the groups of married couples who gathered at Taizé, with whom I spoke about prayer in their lives. So it is to them that I dedicate these pages, as a sign of friendship in the reciprocity of our different vocations.

Frère Pierre-Yves Emery
Taizé, France

PRAYER AT THE HEART OF LIFE

1

Is God alien to us?

The approach to the theme of this chapter was furnished by several married couples who were asked: Why don't worldly commitments and our presence before God in prayer fit together more easily?

It is often said today that prayer—its words and its spiritual attitude—is not adapted to the conditions of real life. Certainly faith must allow all its modes of expression to be reexamined constantly. This is especially true in times of great change.

One notes, however, in the following statements, how these couples do not question prayer as much as they question the world in which they live and the conditions of their human actions. This is very significant. Many persons, especially some Christians, actually seem to think that one's inner life and the spiritual dimension should be accommodated to the rhythms and the climate that society would impose. So a basic question must be put: is the criterion of truth by which we decipher the meaning of life to be the world or Jesus Christ?

Certainly we must be realistic. We must not only

accept but be grateful for the fact that the language of faith, especially prayer, has to be adapted according to the changes in mentality resulting from the transformation of history. But the adaptation will not be in one direction only. We must also ask how we are to understand ourselves and all things in order for our lives to receive meaning in relationship to God. Further, we must ask ourselves what choices we have to make to prevent this relationship—the listening of faith, prayer—from being ejected from our existence. That would be little more than pure conformism to the ambiance and pressures of the consumer society.

Reflections of Some Couples

"Efficiency marks everything in life today, and we must participate, although it is opposed to the idea of doing something for nothing."

"The security with which we surround our lives also estranges us from that gratuitous act which is prayer."

"Rapid change and the resulting superficiality of relationships make it more and more difficult to see the image of Christ in one's neighbor."

"The economic situation today (in Western countries), in which advertising strives to create new needs, develops in us without our realizing it a perpetual feeling of dissatisfaction and unfulfilled desires, which are hardly praiseworthy."

"Socialization: man is increasingly dependent upon a group; one-to-one contacts become less important; individuality disappears in favor of the group. In the relationship with God, it isn't God who lacks reality, neither is it faith in him; it is man himself who seems to disappear. We see the same difficulty in marriage when a person brings home his or her professional worries. The individual gets lost behind his function in society. The relationship with God of this social being (who is shaping the civilization of tomorrow) is yet to be invented."

"Rather than the death of God, we observe the death of man as we have known him. Faith consists in believing in his resurrection."

"The contemplative presence before God is foreign to this superficial and hurried life, in which one spends his time longing for the past while impatient for the future, because today passes too quickly."

"A lack of faith: God does not occupy the primary place, which we ought to reserve for him. We must also admit that sometimes we doubt his 'competence' to handle our worldly problems."

And this remark, which is a good summary of the preceding ones: "For us the universe has been emptied of its spiritual meaning."

So we must note carefully that the problem of prayer today may rest far less in prayer itself than in the meaning we give to the world and to life. Is it our prayer that is apart from real life? Isn't it rather that our life unfolds and is understood apart from prayer?

Prayer: an Alienation?

In times past, prayer itself has not been a problem; the issues were kinds of prayer, its discipline, its control, or its perseverance. Today that has changed. While we share in the modern mentality and the questioning which goes along with it, we must at least satisfy ourselves on the meaning and authenticity of prayer.

The great questions assail us from without and from within. Isn't prayer an alienation of our human freedom? Isn't it a supernatural parenthesis in our natural, human life? Isn't it time wasted or stolen from our presence in the world? Doesn't prayer come from projecting our fears, our desires, and our infantile need for power into some imaginary heaven?

Such questions, behind which are Marxism, Freudian analysis, and the processes of secularization, must first lead us into a purifying consideration about ourselves: does our own experience of prayer deserve these criticisms? More profoundly, these challenges should lead us to establish prayer within a reflection of faith, so that prayer appears as the very opposite of alienation and escape, or attitudes unworthy of an adult. Otherwise we shall not be able to pray seriously, with the energy, conviction, and time that are required.

The Scientific Method

"For us the universe has been emptied of its spiritual meaning." Certainly, science and technology have taught us to experience the world as having its own consistency, an internal coherence, and a harmony of laws which can be known, anticipated, and often modified. The universe seems to be autonomous, developing out of itself. In consequence, current theology refuses to place God among the laws that rule the universe, to use him as a stopgap to explain phenomena that are not yet understood.

What is true of the universe is also true of man. This truth is experienced in mankind's increasing power, its immense responsibility, its freedom, as well as in the weight of its history. This is the autonomy of mankind, in a relative sense at least, and the coherence of the psychological and sociological processes that fashion it.

If we neither can nor wish to locate God among created things, as a stopgap or as someone who intervenes among physical causes on their own level, then where shall we place him? At the limits of man and the world, in the distance? As complementary rather than necessary, since the world and mankind have a consistency and a certain autonomy of their own? If this is so, prayer will, at best, seem accidental, coincidental, without existential foundation, an accessory to life, an alienation.

Without in any way detracting from science's value and possibilities and without disowning the intellectual attitude that science requires, we must accept the importance of not making it a new myth. This grows from respect for what science is. Science is not the only approach to reality, for the simple reason that the method of science is abstraction, the use of statistics, and the artificial separating out from all reality the area chosen for investigation. This is perfectly legitimate if one does not forget that, since it proceeds from abstraction, scientific knowledge remains partial and limited. In particular, the scientific method abstracts God from reality, an abstraction that is legitimate and necessary. But

7

science should not overtly take this methodological principle for a scientific conclusion. Science has nothing to say about God because it disqualifies itself at the outset.

God—Source and Sun

Let us now try to move from a scientific, and therefore abstract, conception of man to that direct, mysterious, existential awareness which we can have of ourselves. It is with something of an élan, a projection, or a desire made of a thousand desires that we know ourselves. There is something almost insatiable about it: a taste not only to have all, but to be all. As adults, we have controlled this impulse, but the child in us is never entirely dead. We are insatiable and, therefore, we are always a bit disappointed, even if we dare not admit it.

In any case, we do not exist simply within ourselves. We are stretched toward something far beyond. I know myself as a specific, indivisible expression, which is myself and my own. And yet that self has been given to me because it has been shaped by my interpersonal relationships. I have received myself from other persons, and to a great extent I continue to receive myself through others. Without others, I would have only the appearance of a human being. I would never have become conscious of myself; I would not have become a person.

Everyone is able to recognize this fact if he reflects on his own intimate experience of himself. What relationship does faith have with this human experience? This, I suggest, leads us to the heart of the question posed in the title of this chapter.

8

Faith is not something added in some external way to what we experience within ourselves. Our belonging to God is not superimposed onto what we already might be by ourselves and within ourselves. No! But faith permits us to name by its true name that élan which radically constitutes us, which indeed we *are*: a calling forth, a vocation of God. As human persons we *are* a vocation, a call to be. We are this élan, which is not God but which is the act and presence of God at the root of our creation and at the goal to which it aims. The very insatiability of this élan reveals the polarity within it: the fullness of God, always beyond all our desires.

God's immanence and transcendence: these are scholarly expressions for the fact that God is simultaneously within and beyond the élan or the calling that defines us. He is within this projection which constitutes us and utterly beyond that expectation for wholeness of being which characterizes us. God is both our inner source and the sun whose shining rays envelop us. "For with thee is the fountain of life; in thy light do we see light" (Ps. 36:9).

"You have created us for yourself," wrote Saint Augustine, "and our heart knows no rest until it rests in you."[1] And Calvin: "We are not our own . . . . We are God's; let all the parts of our life strive toward him as our only lawful goal."[2]

This is certainly affirmation of man's dependence on God, but not of man's alienation. As Genuyt has said: "This dependence is that of a source, not a subjection"; God in Christ is not a "given" that would limit our freedom, but a "Giving" that stirs it up, calls it forth, and renews it.[3]

Man as a self-contained being, subsisting and becoming on his own, is an abstraction that is methodologically legitimate and necessary for the sciences of mankind. These sciences delineate one aspect of reality. But if, to know where we are existentially and really in relationship to God and to ourselves, we begin by describing ourselves as self-contained beings, subsisting by ourselves, then God can only seem our limit, and we his, in juxtaposition and even insoluble rivalry. He becomes a counterfeit God, unreal, the anti-image of a partial and counterfeit image of ourselves. Actually, we have no reason to demand of or defend before God that relative autonomy of creation, in particular man's self-subsistence, which science has made the object of its study. God has willed it and does not cease to promote it.

Concerned about separating God from his creation, and wishing to venerate his greatness, we Christians have probably emphasized the transcendence of God in a unilateral way: God as absolute other. To that we must add our almost insurmountable difficulty in thinking of God as someone we meet face to face, without limiting him to a being who is only face to face with us. We almost inevitably project onto God our own experience of what it means to be persons, with all our human limitations.

However, beyond the limits which we experience in ourselves and which we more or less consciously ascribe to God, and also beyond our fear of seeing others limit our freedom—and God risks being an "other" for us—a more searching reflection on what "others" really are helps us see that God does not stand beyond us as a limit. Thus, a true relationship of love or friendship between two human persons, even if it is never perfect or total, enables us to see that people do not simply exist side by side but mutually enter into each other's lives and belong to each other. As I pointed out earlier, whatever we are is revealed to us and in a way is given to us by those who for us are *persons*; moreover, it is through concern for and the giving of ourselves to those persons that we become more fully ourselves. This human experience, especially that of a married couple, can help us understand in what sense a relationship with God, in which we receive from him absolutely and ceaselessly, can be not an alienation but rather a freedom and a way to freedom.

The Infinity of a Presence

Often in Christian thought, the fear of a certain vitalism (which limits God to an impersonal, determinist élan) or an embryonic pantheism (which confuses God with the universe) makes us conceive of God's transcendence as something exterior and alien. Further, the wish to emphasize grace as a free gift allows us to think of it as somehow tangential to the world and to mankind and, in the end, as arbitrary. If we then overexaggerate the novel and unexpected nature of redemption, we may end up thinking it has only an occasional or accidental relationship with creation. But if the plan of God is not grasped in its unity, man seems to be burdened with choosing between being a creature or being saved,

11

between belonging to the world or belonging to God. One or the other has to be considered an alienation.

But God is not external to the being that he created. Granted he is the "wholly other" beyond our every intellectual or imaginative representation; our creaturely condition binds us to time and space whereas God dominates time and space infinitely. But to say that, in relationship to us, God is the "wholly other" is still speaking from our condition as creatures. God is, in fact, even more other than that which we call other. That is why he is not "purely other" but rather is "wholly other than other."[4] A single thing equals the difference and the infinite distance between God and us: the intimate presence of the Creator at the heart of his creation.

So the transcendence of God is not an elsewhere, an absence. "The beyond is not that which is infinitely distant, but that which is most near . . . . It is at the heart of our life that God is beyond" (Dietrich Bonhoeffer),[5] at the center of our reality as its source and its dimension of infinity. "The God of Jesus Christ is the real at its source" (André Manaranche).[6] "He is the Ground of all Being, always present in all, always creating and destroying, always understood to be as close to us as we are to ourselves, yet at the same time always inaccessible . . . the Ground and Meaning of all Being" (Paul Tillich).[7]

Therefore we falsify reality, we put ourselves in an impossible situation, and we lose sight of the meaning of prayer (and more generally of the meaning of our relationship with God) if we understand the transcendence of God in too human and simplistic a manner, as a distance, and external. That distance or that external becomes for us either a strangeness (and our life in the world obviously has no more relationship with prayer) or a usurped authority (and all human existence, including prayer, appears as an alienation).

Very differently, revelation leads us to confess the immensity of God in close connection with his presence in the world and, better still, his immensity as the dimension of his presence in everything that receives being from him.

"Transcendence, if it is the transcendence of the God of our faith, cannot exclude the condescendence and familiarity of God, and vice versa" (Yves Congar).[8] "In biblical or Christian language transcendence does not mean something completely beyond or situated outside of history, but its immanent achievement" (J.B. Metz).[9]

So God is at the heart of the world and its history, of men's persons and man's history. But he is not enclosed there. On the contrary, the creature is open to the infinite otherness of God. As Saint Hilary has said, God "keeps himself at the interior and the exterior of everything. His infinity cannot be absent from any part, and nothing is able to escape from him who is infinite."[10]

And Karl Barth has made this charming remark: "Time itself is in eternity. Its whole extensions, from beginning to end, every epoch, every lifetime, every new and closing year, every passing hour: they are all in eternity like a child in the arms of its mother."[11]

13

Saint Paul said (quoting some Greek philosophers): "In him we live and move and have our being . . . for we are indeed his offspring," (Acts 17:28). Not only at the beginning, but continually, all that we are, all that we perceive through senses and spirit, all that we do is mysteriously enveloped by and rooted in the creative will of God, is expressed by his Word. So for man, being and being-in-God are not separable; still less can they oppose each other in such a way that being-in-God would alienate a part of our being. For God, the meaning of men's lives is engraved upon them from their beginning: "Yet for us there is one God, the Father, from whom are all things and for whom we exist" (1 Cor. 8:6).

The Beauty of the World?

Why is this cosmic dimension of faith, this perception of the world as a creation of God more difficult for us today? We have already seen that the intellectual climate, stimulated by the scientific method, leads us more and more to consider the universe in itself and for itself, as a "given" that carries within itself all the laws and energy for its evolution.

But isn't there another reason? It has become less customary for us to praise God for the beauty of the world and the marvel that man is. That custom seems sentimental and romantic in attitude, a way of cheapening the tragedy and misery that mark life in the world, a sidestepping of man's responsibility.

We see less the beauty of the world than its incompleteness and the evil that is in it. The grace of

14

being human impresses us less than the limits and guilt that mark human life. It is the same with the other works of God. The grace of the Church nearly disappears because of the flaws and blemishes that we see. And even Scripture often seems to be less a blessing than a mountain of problems of interpretation.

We look at everything critically. And there is nothing wrong in that, but we must ask what motivates and directs the criticism. For if criticism is without appreciation, if it proceeds from suspicion rather than from wonder, it debases itself. Criticism then is no longer the desire to understand more clearly, but is a covert effort at self-defense; it is corrosion rather than attention. It is nothing but a form of self-justification, a bitter and derisive comfort for those who surrender to the delirium of persecution, wall themselves in, and die little by little.

Neither God without Man, nor Man without God

The incarnation of Jesus Christ shows and witnesses to us that God has not wished to be without man nor to make himself known to us other than as God united with man, Emmanuel. Nothing required this of him, but it is the way he manifests his freedom.

Since the incarnation *and in consequence of it,* we can no longer think of man without God, nor can we know ourselves otherwise than as images of God, called to resemble him in a communion, a "divinization" as the Orthodox put it, which is no less than the very freedom of man and that fullness to which he aspires with all of his being.

But how can we fix this conviction at the center of our concrete, immediate self-consciousness, rather than alongside it? We must see Christ's incarnation, in its newness and grace, as the consequence and as the renewal of that first manifestation of God's love, his creation.

Creation and Salvation

Why is it important for us to synthesize Christ's incarnation and the creation of the world? Because our prayer responds to the movement by which God has come to us and inserts itself within the movement by which Christ leads us back to the Father through his death and resurrection. In other words, our prayer is essentially a result of the coming of Christ, of his incarnation, and of his work of salvation.

Our human action itself locates us in the world, puts us into contact with things, involves us in the immense work of mankind which, throughout history, must prolong creation. To put it another way, our daily action is primarily a consequence of creation. Our consciousness of ourselves is that of persons born into this world; we discover ourselves through our relationships with other persons and the things that surround us.

It is, therefore, extremely important for the coherence of our Christian lives, and for the unity of prayer and daily action within them, to understand clearly that creation and salvation exist *within each other*. The created world is not merely the external frame for the work of our salvation; the coming of Christ to restore us to the Father does not

16

treat the world as simply a place of transition. No, it is truly "to his own home" that the Word has come, to a world where not anything that was made was made without him (John 1:3, 11). We exist—all things exist—only through him (1 Cor. 8:6). In the same movement he is the Word as creator and the Word coming from the Father, as John Scotus, a theologian of the ninth century, said very well: "It is the Word of God that gives and conserves being in the created universe, or in other words, the eternal and immutable generation of his Word."[12]

God has not changed his plan. The Word comes from within to recapture and to bring to fulfillment that which God began by creation and by the physical birth of each person throughout history. This is at the heart of the world and the world lives by it: the Word of God, incarnation itself, becomes one of us and gathers us together in him. By the very act of saving us and reconciling us with the Father, Jesus Christ reveals to us the original meaning of creation and, therefore, the meaning of our lives at the heart of the created world. This meaning is a gift, but it is within a communion, a reciprocity of giving. Our lives and the world in which they participate are *gifts of God* but continue to be so only in becoming *gifts to God*.

Isn't this precisely what Jesus Christ lived among us? Dramatically, it is true, because he lived the freedom of grace at the very heart of our sort of alienation—sin, a spiritual hallucination. Christ thereby recovered the first movement of creation from within. He restored to its original truth that desire for wholeness which characterizes the human being, and he revealed why man becomes lost, falling into meaninglessness and nonbeing, when he seeks to fulfill his life apart from God.

Saint Bernard rightly celebrated the linking of these two works of God, creation and salvation, as the flowering of that unique gift by which man receives himself from God: "In his first work God has given myself to me, and in the second he has given himself, and in giving himself to me, he has given me back myself."[13]

Prayer, Expression of Our Human Truth

When we have recalled this, it is not difficult to grasp the fact that, if prayer is revealed to us by God through the incarnation of his Son as the attitude of a man who lives in communion with God, then it is also the expression of that élan which radically constitutes us as human persons.

This is not to say that true prayer just happens by itself or that we can initiate it by ourselves. But neither is prayer just added onto whatever we are. It is not an attitude that is imposed upon us from outside, limiting our freedom. On the contrary, prayer is simply the recognition of our true identity before God, the truest and deepest expression of our truth and freedom. It causes us to say, along with a medieval author, William of St. Thierry: "Lord, may this good happen to me which is to be in you; I, for whom the worst is to be in myself."[14]

In the same sense, Alexandre Vinet prayed: "It is you, yourself, almighty God, that I ask of you. Your presence, your absence is life or death to me."[15]

Certainly, the call of God through Jesus Christ strikes us as an uprooting from ourselves, and we risk experiencing it as an alienation if we do not see that withdrawal into ourselves is the only real alienation, a withdrawal in which the great desire for being which gives us life falls back onto itself and shatters into a thousand little desires. Then, yes, God seems a demanding Lord who constrains us, struggles with us, and makes us feel guilty. But this is because we did not, in the first place, have the courage to be truly and to the very end what we are: a limitless thirst, an élan that is fulfilled only beyond itself in communion with God.

Do we recognize that we are not made to exist in ourselves and by ourselves? If so, the demand of the gospel immediately seems to fit together exactly with the truth of our being and to liberate our freedom. That truth is ours. We have received it, and we are receiving it: it is God. Seeking God, we find ourselves most truly; at the same time the lordship of God takes on a completely different meaning for us. "You alone are truly Lord, you for whom to dominate us is to save us, while for us to serve you is nothing other than to be saved by you" (William of St. Thierry).[16]

This is why we can affirm with assurance the perfectly *human* truth, which is no less supernatural, of biblical expressions such as: "I have no good apart from thee. . . . The Lord is my chosen portion and my cup" (Ps. 16:2,5). "For to me to live is Christ, and to die is gain" (Phil. 1:21). God is the opposite of all alienation. He is so much the final, secret object of all our most human desires that the psalmist can say to him in a burst of lucidity (which is faith): "Whom have I in heaven but thee? And there is nothing upon earth that I desire besides thee" (Ps. 73:25).

In the same sense, there is a prayer of Saint Bernard that ends with a striking and paradoxical definition of man: "He who refuses to live for you, Lord Jesus, is dead; he who has not dedicated his intelligence to you is irrational; and he who is concerned to exist for anything else but for you exists for nothing and is nothing. In a word, what is man other than the being to whom you have made yourself known?"[17]

But, if we must remember all this in order to establish the human truth of prayer, we must be careful not to conceive of prayer as a final way of searching for ourselves, a way that is more insidious because it is more spiritual. Prayer must be gratuitous. Why? In order not to treat God as a means and thus to misunderstand him and to lose him. Gratuitousness is essential because it constitutes love. But it is not arbitrary on our part; it is merely the attempt to respond to the gratuitousness of the love of God.

The term "gratuitous" here does not signify "for nothing," without a context, without a goal, expecting nothing. That would be not taking God seriously and would be contrary to the truth. Gratuitous, rather, means without calculation, without reservation, expecting nothing except God himself. Saint Augustine said: "Love not God as if you were to be rewarded for it; for your supreme reward will be the presence of God, himself, whom you freely love. And you must love in such a way that you do not cease to desire him as reward, he who alone is able to satisfy you."[18]

"All that is mine is yours," said the father, in the parable, to the elder brother of the prodigal son (Luke 15:31).

If we are finally able to convince ourselves that the truth of God is his ardent desire to share with us all that he is, we will give up our secret thought that, after all, God being God, he must somehow limit us in our desires and our freedom. And we will cease dreaming of little reservations of being and of freedom that we would have to arrange behind his back.

According to a saying of Saint Irenaeus, which is often quoted today, "the glory of God is man fully alive"[19]—and not as a diminished man, crushed, restricted, ceasing to be himself. But this saying carries a second proposition, which is curiously, and revealingly, often forgotten. However, in context, it is the part emphasized. "The glory of man is the vision of God." Man is not his own sun nor the fullness of his own life.

To See God

The Psalms so often express man's desire to see God, to see his face. To see God and, of course, to hear him. (It is understood that these verbs symbolize a reality that is not in the realm of our senses.) To listen to and to hear God is the attitude of faith and obedience, the point of departure all along the route of our Christian life on earth.

To see God is the object of Christian hope in the future, and yet, throughout the Old Testament and even more often in the New Testament in a mysterious half-light, faith already attains that hope. It is a special intimacy that expresses itself in this way, an intimacy of the presence of God and of the presence before God at the heart of faith.

One is able to hear at a distance, but being able to see implies a nearness. In that nearness is the wonder of love, and in that wonder is the transformation of the one who sees into his true being. "Man is when he sees God. He *is* when he sees him who is and, in seeing him who is, he also becomes himself in his own way, in order *to be*," according to Saint Augustine.[20]

To see and to hear God! But let's be clear, in order not to entertain illusions or to deceive ourselves, that these verbs are used as analogues. They express something true and profound; using terms of our sense experience, they point to an experience of another order, that of faith. It is comparable to a blind man saying, "I see." In our experience we are often able to evoke two levels of seeing and hearing. I see someone who passes by, or I see an acquaintance or my wife or child. Physically it is the same optical phenomenon, but in the second case, the seeing is accompanied by a recognition, by a movement of the heart, by an inner sight awakened by the physical sight. And so, facing Christ and in him facing the Father, the inner sight is awakened, not by what our eyes see but by the knowledge of faith, based on the testimony of those who have seen and touched the Word made flesh; based also on certain signs such as the sacraments or the love of neighbor, and awakened in us by the Holy Spirit.

* * * * *

In a word, today more than ever, these two things are to be held together and affirmed together: God is truly the object of our desire for being and fullness; but God does not subject himself to our wishes. A double danger threatens us: imagining God as being external to us, distant and alienating; or making God a dimension and a projection of ourselves.

The desire for God in us must constantly go beyond itself and must convert itself into the desire of God, in a movement by which that desire, without ceasing to be ours, lets itself be filled and transfigured by God.

NOTES

1. Augustine, *Confessions*, I, 1.

2. John Calvin, *Institutes of the Christian Religion* (1545), ed. John T. McNeill, Library of Christian Classics XX (Philadelphia: Westminster, 1960), p. 690.

3. François Marie Genuyt, "Approche philosophique de la vie religieuse," *Lumière et Vie* 96 (January–February 1970) 103.

4. Hans Urs von Balthasar, *L'Amour seul est digne de foi* (Paris 1966), p. 66.

5. Dietrich Bonhoeffer, *Résistance et soumission* (Geneva 1967), p. 184.

6. André Manaranche, *Y a-t-il une éthique sociale chrétienne?* (Paris 1969), p. 176.

7. Paul Tillich, *Jewish Influences on Contemporary Christian Theology,* trans. George Tavard in *Initiation à Paul Tillich* (Paris 1968), p. 55.

8. Yves Congar, "Dum visibiliter Deum cognoscimus," in *Les voies du Dieu vivant* (Paris: Du Cerf, 1962), p. 96.

9. J.B. Metz, *L'anthropocentrique chrétienne* (Paris 1968), p. 120.

10. Hilary, *On the Trinity,* I, 6.

11. Karl Barth, *Church Dogmatics,* trans. T.H.L. Parker, W.B. Johnston, *et al;* ed G.W. Bromley and T.F. Torrance (Edinburgh: Clark and New York: Scribners, 1957), Vol. II, Part 1, p. 623.

12. John Scotus, *Homily on the Prologue of St. John,* ch. 18.

13. Bernard, *Treatise on the Love of God,* V, 15.

14. William of St. Thierry, *Contemplation of God,* 5.

15. Alexandre Vinet, *Louange et prière,* No. 190.

16. William of St. Thierry, *op. cit.,* 9.

17. Bernard, *On the Canticle,* Sermon 20, 1.

18. Augustine, *Commentaries on the Psalms,* 134, 11.

19. Irenaeus, *Against the Heresies,* IV, 20, 7.

20. Augustine, *Commentaries, op. cit.,* 121, 8.

2

Is prayer foreign to life?

The preceding chapter was a detour necessary to approach the theme of this chapter. It was necessary to recall the infinite presence of God in the world, the divine logic that ties together creation and salvation, and the meaning of our life and of our freedom as a movement toward God, in order to be able to discuss the meaning and the place of prayer in a life that seeks to be fully human, involved in earthly tasks and in the brotherhood of mankind.

I am not forgetting that the purpose of these meditations is the question of many Christians today—a question that is also often an objection: Is prayer not juxtaposed against life as an accessory that has no meaning, or perhaps even as an escape from reality, an alienation? In the preceding pages I have already more than intimated that the opposition between prayer and human life on earth is not an opposition *in principle*. Man's knowledge of God and of himself, which is deciphered in Christ, shows that this objection involves an error in perspective.

It is nonetheless true that in our personal experience, prayer and human life may seem to be juxtaposed. So we now turn to asking why it is necessary to avoid such a juxtaposition, and how we can strive to surmount it.

Precise Terminology

In this connection, notice that I do not say "prayer and life." That would seem to put prayer outside life and falsely limit life to certain other activities. Neither do I say "prayer and commitment," for in the language of today's Christians "commitment" generally suggests too exclusively those activities which are taken on in addition to habitual tasks. I prefer to use the phrase "prayer and human action."

Of course prayer is, in its own way, also an action, and the adjective "human" indicates the duties and the freedoms that a Christian assumes alongside and in the same way as other people on earth. The term "action" is general enough to include the primary responsibilities of a married man and woman—home and children—as well as the responsibilities of every adult in his vocation, which is both a way of making a living and a participation in the life and development of mankind. The term also covers friendly and social relationships, participation in the Church, involvement in society, political responsibilities, concern to keep informed and to grow culturally, choice of leisure activities. In short, the word covers everything from the most highly organized to the most unpredictable—and through all runs the desire to witness to the gospel.

As to "prayer," I do not envisage it primarily as the words that express it, or as the forms it takes

—praise, intercession, repentance—but more generally as a conscious attitude of presence and attention before God.

Two Possible Dangers

There are two opposing dangers. Out of concern for human brotherhood, or in order to be involved fully in the movement of secularization, or simply as justification for the neglect of prayer, one runs the risk of giving human action such a privileged place that it seems to absorb prayer. Thus some people say, "my life and my commitment are my prayer." There is some truth to that statement because it refuses to allow a dichotomy in Christian life. Yet there is also much possible illusion. How can there be a conscious waiting for God that does not take a particular form, as such? It is essential that we strive to make all our lives a presence before God, but to affirm too quickly that they already are can be dangerous and, perhaps, somewhat naive and pretentious.

The other danger, less frequent in our age, is that of exalting prayer so that human action takes on a purely utilitarian function, regrettable but necessary and without much relationship to God: one has to live, but this world is only a sort of waiting room for the Kingdom. This attitude sets the prayer of Mary and her choice of the "better part" against the action of Martha. It is true that the unique meaning of prayer is expressing choice of the "one thing necessary"—Christ. But prayer loses its meaning and its nature, and it denies the incarnation if it seems to disqualify our life in the world.

27

In the Gospel story (Luke 10:38–42), it is not the prayer of Mary that is opposed to the work of Martha. Neither is the mysticism of one set against the realism of the other. It is the attention Mary pays to the presence of Jesus that is opposed to the agitation of Martha and to her preoccupation with tasks, a preoccupation not oriented and ordered in relation to his presence. It is perfectly clear that prayer is not the only way to be attentive to God and to love him, but it is no less clear that human action is not, in itself, attention to God.

This second danger, that of underrating the world and human action in the name of prayer, is rare today, even though it is frequently denounced. But what is not rare is the inability of many persons to believe in the meaning of their jobs. This is not because of prayer but because of the economic and social conditions of their work. This can be a very serious obstacle to prayer. But I merely note it here because I will take up this subject again in the appendix at the end of this chapter.

Now, in order to approach intelligently the subtle relationship between prayer and human action, a relationship that neither suppresses the differences nor tolerates a separation, we must discuss two major New Testament themes: man created in God's image, and the Kingdom as the central object of Jesus' message.

Christ as Image

In all his life on earth, Christ is simultaneously the image of God for man, and *the image of man before God*. (I stress *of man before God* because viewing man in himself is an abstraction, and that is not the way in which Jesus is man.) In other words, Christ reveals who God is for man: he for whom and by whom man exists, God essentially united with man. But Christ equally reveals the concrete image to which man refers and through which man must approach in order to enter into communion with the Father. This has always been the true meaning of man's existence, the *raison d'être* of his life. Mankind had lost sight of it, and God reveals it and reconstitutes it through his Son: created in the image of God, man was "predestined to be conformed to the image of his Son" (Rom. 8:29).

To bring ourselves close to this image by working toward an authentic resemblance is the goal of that desire *to be* which constitutes us so basically. We can also say that "image" describes all our earthly existence with its manifold activity. Following Christ, conforming our lives to his, consists of wishing to continue and to actualize his work through all our human tasks. Our image, the life of Christ incarnate, present in the world, in brotherhood with humanity, servant through love, is, therefore, necessarily concerned with our human actions.

At the same time, this theme of image immediately calls forth prayer. Following Christ, seeking to refer all our lives to his earthly life, is also joining him through faith in his resurrection; it is following him with our hearts into his glory at the right hand of God, where our "life is hid with Christ in God" (Col. 3:1). It is seeking, scrutinizing, and loving his countenance.

We can, therefore, say that fundamentally all our

action, on one hand, and our prayer, on the other, can both be defined as quest for the face of Christ, in order to resemble him. Prayer and human action are mutually self-inclusive in this effort.

The Kingdom Come and Yet to Come

The theme of the Kingdom very directly concerns our human action, for, in one sense, the announcement of the Kingdom addresses itself to all men and to the whole man. It is not a skimming off of souls but a harvesting of the world and its history, through a mysterious transfiguration which today seems to us like an enormous and painful birth (Rom. 8:19 ff). In another sense, the announcement of the Kingdom reveals God to us as anything but passive. "My Father is working still, and I am working," said Jesus (John 5:17). In our human action, the Kingdom mobilizes us as a vast labor force of God; it builds itself through our work, our responsibilities and our involvements, and our most diverse human commitments, to the extent that our action brings about a reconciliation among men and a harmony between mankind and the universe.

Nevertheless, the Kingdom is not the fruit of history. It does not germinate from "below." It is not the idealization of our politics or our economics. The Kingdom, as eternal life, consists essentially in knowing the true God and the one he has sent, Jesus Christ (John 17:3). The Kingdom is given from "above" in the coming of Christ. That is why the theme of the Kingdom expressly concerns and calls forth prayer, as expectation of the Kingdom and as affirmation that the Kingdom comes in Christ and that it is communion with the Father.

We see, therefore, the outline of the intimate correlation between prayer and human action: the Kingdom requires our action because Christ has come and because his work is built through our lives. That same unique Kingdom requires our prayer because Christ is coming, and we await his reign as a grace, or rather as the fullness of grace.

We may legitmately describe life in the glory of the Kingdom as the absolute disappearance of all differences between prayer and action. Then we will be able to say that action is prayer and prayer is existence. Meanwhile, a distinction remains, and even a certain concrete tension exists between prayer and human action. We try to surmount or to reduce this tension, but we are never able to here below because the Kingdom which has come is also still to come.

We must remember this fact in order to avoid both the false juxtaposition and the short-circuiting of prayer and human action.

Being and Doing

We have to admit, however, that prayer, considered as a specific activity, a time set apart, an explicit concentration of all one's being, does seem to be something separate. So what? That does not make it an escape or a betrayal of the earth. All our action, in fact all life, is composed of specific activities that follow one after the other and are more or less separate, more or less linked.[1] Our capacity to do several things at once is rather limited; when we try, the intensity of our involvement in each thing diminishes proportionately.

But below the level of getting our activities underway, of "doing," is another hidden level, which is that of "being." This is our basic attitude, the overall aim of life and of the meaning that we see in it. This is where the unity between prayer and the rest of life can operate. Cut off from that deeper level of being, human action becomes vanity, and prayer is nothing more than words.

Toward Reciprocity

So that prayer and action can nourish each other, one can underscore with Bishop Robinson[2] the importance of discovering God with, in, and among the events of daily life. One is then able to practice an instantaneous and frequent prayer which, without interrupting activity or hindering contact with one's neighbor, presents all to God, in order to live under his gaze.

But one also needs to be concerned about knowing how prayer and human action—as separate activities—relate to each other. For neither the discovery of God in daily life nor instantaneous prayer can bypass a set time spent in the presence of God. Rather they demand such a time, in order not to become illusions.

In fact, prayer cannot develop from pure spontaneity. Nothing of value in life comes into being without a passion reflected and concentrated in perseverance, experience, and habits. Without the gift of ourselves and of that which has become very precious to us—our time—will not prayer simply start tending toward zero?

I will try to suggest, in two stages, the meaning and role of prayer in relation to human action, and

32

then the meaning and role of that action in relation to prayer. As a preamble, let me emphasize that this effort is not intended to establish the *raison d' être* of either prayer or action, nor to reduce them to a utilitarian function. The meaning of work is not limited to earning money, the aim of rest is not merely to recover strength for more work; sexual union is not only for purposes of procreation, likewise, prayer does not aim essentially at the deepening of our human commitments. Work, rest, love, and prayer do not receive their value from one another but from the fact that each of them, in its own way, is the expression of a person who recognizes himself as part of the grace of God—although not without difficulty.

PRAYER AT THE HEART OF ACTION

The dimension and the meaning that faith gives to man's life in the world may be described, as we have seen, as the direction to follow in joining Christ, man's image, or as an involvement in the coming of the Kingdom, or as a way of receiving God and of giving oneself to him.

A Recentering

Practically speaking, however, human action, with its diversity, its varied techniques, the way it limits and concentrates attention, its own laws which dictate the nature of things and the resistance of other persons, is not, of itself, dedicated to God or attentive to him. Far from it! Efficiency imposes objective limits, interrelated and extremely diver-

33

sified. Life itself scatters man's attention, even when it most obviously has meaning only in relation to God, as in the work of a clergyman or theologian. The unexpected comes up all the time, events absorb our energy, and soon we run the risk of losing the thread of life's meaning.

These facts, which are in no way peculiar to Christians, are not tragic. Such is reality. It is normal that life spreads us thin. Recognizing this helps us understand that it is not a luxury but a profound necessity for every person to find regular occasions during which, by re-entering into himself and taking a second look he can recover the thread of his life and find some coherence for his diverse actions.

In this sense, for the Christian, prayer appears not as a parenthesis or as a simple moment of respite, but as a *recentering of the person and of its action in respect to its image.*

So much more since this image is not an outline which requires merely a glance once in a while. It is the countenance of Christ, the face whose features we find running through all the events of Jesus' earthly life according to the gospel, the face of the resurrected one, a face that demands contemplation for itself, in love.

And that contemplation, Saint Paul has told us, implies a patient, inner transformation, a conversion. In order to see Christ it is first necessary to look for him and to receive from the Holy Spirit the freedom to drop the veil from our eyes, so that our own face is disclosed. We are then able, with eyes of faith, not only to see but to reflect the light of Christ

34

which is the glory of God and "to be changed into his likeness from one degree of glory to another" (2 Cor. 3:18).

It is, therefore, clear that attention to Christ, the looking within to discern Christ's face, is not merely the privilege of a few souls who have the taste for it. Rather it is the condition and the heart of any life that seeks to be Christian, of human action that seeks to be undertaken in faithful reference to Christ.

A Way of Looking at the World

In addition, the prayer that recenters existence in contemplation of Christ contemplates, from that point, human realities, in order to perceive and grasp them in their profound value and eternal meaning, rather than in their superficial appearance. How can the image of Christ become the pole of my daily existence, how can I live an authentic presence in the world if I do not strive, in prayer, as the apostle said, to "look not to the things that are seen but to the things that are unseen; for the things that are seen are transient, but the things that are unseen are eternal" (2 Cor. 4:18)? The "unseen" is not to be understood here as another realm superimposed on that of the real world. The concrete is not to be abandoned in favor of the abstract; rather the visible reality is to be seen in its depth and spiritual meaning, in its tie to God. According to Claudel: "We do not really look at things if we do not see their cause, which is God,"[3] and Bonhoeffer: "All things appear distorted if they are not seen and recognized in God."[4]

Far from limiting man's presence in the world, such prayer is the authority for the truth of that presence and must, if possible, prevent it from degrading itself into a worldly conformism. Presence in the world is not an end in itself, and the world is not the ultimate point of reference. It is presence in the world *of God,* in the world called to be harvested in the Kingdom. God himself is first of all truly present in the world, and only through presence before God can man hope to know how to be present in the world with him, following Christ. Can anyone measure the lucidity of insight which that presupposes? Or the unstable equilibrium and near contradiction which that implies? Oppenheimer remarked prophetically: "We face times in which it will be difficult to keep our minds open and our spirits deep."[5]

For the Christian, presence in the world is the difficult road toward an authentic freedom, the freedom in God. As the sociologist Gaston Berger said: "A true involvement in the world, the sort one speaks too much about and which is very fashionable, must be the decision of a free spirit. But it is necessary first to attain freedom; otherwise we are not involved in the world, we are lost in it."[6]

I could continue in this vein about the Christians today who show such a striking concern about clearly recognizing the secularity of the world and its own consistency. For prayer, as explicit attention to God, does not contradict true secularization; rather it is one of its conditions. The great danger, in fact, is that the more radical the secularization, the more the created world is made into an absolute, an ultimate end, thus covertly making it something sacred and divine, as if it existed only of and for itself. This is why it is so important for the world itself and all its action to be consecrated to God, to be turned toward the Kingdom. In order to de-mythologize the world truly, it must be seen and lived as having meaning only with reference to the summing up of all creation in Christ.[7]

The Ambiguities of Commitment

Perhaps all this has been presented in too ideal a way. I am thinking especially of Christians whose commitment to politics, social causes, and labor unions is especially risky and demanding. In order to be effective and realistic, a person's involvement in the service of others is necessarily limited. But this often leaves him with the discouraging impression of being only a drop in the ocean. And if his own involvement appears to him the only important one and in his eyes disqualifies the choices and actions of other people, he is just consoling himself for the little bit that he can do.

There is more. Such commitments, and the responsibilities they bring, are necessarily limited on all sides by other persons' conscious or unconscious resistance, often even by their ill will and the whole complex gamut of agressiveness. So one finds oneself unavoidably enmeshed in sinful situations which render ambiguous the most generous options, the options most concerned with justice and truth. The great temptation then is to try to avoid the pangs of conscience, either by escaping from the options or by calling evil good. Then a denial of God is already taking root.

Humility constantly runs the danger of degenerating into self-contempt and scorn for what one is able to do, self-assurance degenerates into pride, efficient realism beats down spiritual exigencies, all of which bring about a perpetually bad conscience.

So it is always necessary for our attention to rest squarely on Christ, not as a solution to all of the problems of our action, but as the one who restores us to action; his Kingdom is both the horizon of our involvements and their internal dynamism. Then our action, with all its limits and ambiguities, is able, by the same movement in which we present it to Christ, to appear to us as humble but not discouraging, inserted into a vast brotherhood of which Christ is the head.

Furthermore, we must present to Christ our bad conscience, our disappointment, our shame, for the forgiveness of the guilt resulting from the ambiguity of our wordly choices and their realization. Only as we agree to be *relative* to Christ does it become possible for us to accept the *relativity* of our human condition without falling into passive resignation.

The Risk of Losing Heart

All those who have public functions, in the secular world or in the Church, and all those who have a responsibility for management, with all the failures, criticisms, and temptations which that implies, should read what Saint Bernard wrote to the pope.[8]

38

A certain distance, a spiritual break is a vital necessity if one is not to lose heart—in the various meanings of the term.

I am afraid that, surrounded by occupations so numerous that you despair of getting through them, you crease your forehead and thus gradually deprive yourself in a way of that good which the suffering of this office can do you. It would be far more prudent of you to back off at times from all this, rather than to permit it unavoidably and step by step to drag you to go where you do not wish to go. Do you ask where? I reply; to a *hard heart.* Do not further ask what that means, for if you do not fear it with trembling, your heart is already hard.

There is no heart more hard than that which does not shudder at the hardness which it cannot feel. Why ask me? Ask Pharaoh instead. No one with a hard heart was ever able to receive salvation, unless God in his compassion removed his heart of stone and gave him a heart of flesh, as the prophet said (Ezek. 36:26).

What then is a hard heart? It is one which is not moved by repentance, which is not softened by piety, nor moved by prayer. It does not yield to threats, but hardens itself under blows. It is ungrateful for blessings, does not listen to good counsel, is irritated in judging, without scruples in shame, without a sense of fear in the midst of danger, without humanity toward human realities, thinking that anything goes with regard to divine realities. It forgets the past, neglects the present, and does not foresee the future. For it, there is no past which is not completely past except wrongs, nothing present that does not perish, and for the future nothing foreseen and prepared except perhaps some work of vengeance.

In brief, to sum up the mischief of this dreadful evil, it is a heart which neither fears God nor respects man. Note well therefore where these wretched occupations will take you, if you persist in giving yourself wholly to them, without keeping something of you for yourself. You are wasting time and if I may permit someone to speak in my place, Jethro (Exod. 18:18), you are also going to consume yourself at the price of unthinkable pain, in these tasks which do not come without torture of spirit, the enfeebling of the mind, and the voiding of grace. What is the fruit of all this, if not spider webs?

Discerning Grace

Viewing reality in its depth and probing its invisible meaning—I mentioned this theme before, but I want to insist on it. Prayer as attention to God, at the heart of our lives, is indispensable if we are to discern the work of God for us and around us in the Church, in the world, in the attitude of this or that person.

Instinctively we are more sensitive to that which fails than that which succeeds. The newspapers are full of bad news; people rarely speak of good news. More than many others, our age is one of criticism, and from an incontestable intellectual method, this criticism tends to develop into a collective psychological reflex. Beneath the seriousness and lucidity of the man who does not want to be "taken in" are sometimes hidden the reactions of a spoiled child. Is it truly intelligent, truly realistic to consider the pains and irritations of life as catastrophes, and to regard as absolutely normal and our due everything good that happens? We will not escape this pseudo-lucidity without another vision, that of attention to God. Not in order to hide our eyes from evil; on the contrary, we shall see it more clearly. But we shall no longer see only evil.

Positive realities, good news, are infinitely more difficult to discern. It is a fact of experience that it always takes much more time and effort to build than to destroy. A tree brings its fruit to maturity by imperceptible progress, through small efforts undertaken with great patience; so also does love grow to fidelity or peace become established in a corner of the world. Yet in one blow all can be destroyed. Further, not to see the good and rejoice in it is already to begin to destroy it. Our criticism must arm itself with great prudence and self-criticism.

Moreover, the law that rules the realities of earth is the same for God's action. In his dealings with men, God regularly chooses those things which are hidden, weak, and apparently insignificant in this world as the channels of his activity and as the proof of his love. Before unbridled evil, the grace and fruits that we allow him to bring to us never seem to measure up sufficiently. We are baffled and scandalized every time. This scandal explains, to a great extent, the "God is dead" theology; it is carried to an extreme within a civilization that so firmly believes in the power of technology, with its striking successes, its explosions of various kinds, and its immediate results.

The scandal, therefore, is a God who does not seem to measure up, and the feelings of abandonment, failure, secret shame of self and of God, open

41

aggression against the Church. Hasn't evil won the field? Or is it our error in wishing that grace would use the same methods as evil, letting technology determine the terrain and the measures—along with the publicity? Not, of course, that technology is evil. Technology can serve grace and love. But love itself is not of the order of technology; its power is not measured by the same norms.

Rather, we are advised that the power of God deploys itself in weakness (2 Cor. 12:9), can be compared to the germination of a seed and not to the explosion of a bomb. It manifests itself where one least expects it and, above all, in ways one would hardly imagine. Unless there is a constantly renewed attention to God and to prayer, which, beginning with God, helps us take the true measure of things, we shall continue to overlook grace and its fruits in men and continue to see only human defeats and the apparent passivity of God.

Over and over we are tempted to separate the cross of Christ from his resurrection, seeing the cross as a defeat followed by a victory. It is important that we continually rediscover the indissoluble unity between the cross and the resurrection, the unity of one and the same event. The love of Christ and his freedom make his death itself a victory over death, over evil, over ignominy. And it is of this victory that resurrection is the manifestation.

It is the same for us. The victories we dream of will always be vain if we wish to avoid having them happen within us through the cross—in other words, through a love that transfigures the shadows. We shall go from unreality to self-deception if we do not see that the limitations and defeat that mark our enterprises can be, without masochism on our part, the mysterious road and almost a necessary condition to our success.

In Summary

This is the meaning of prayer at the heart of life and human action; in prayer, life recognizes itself as a gift of God and as a gift to God, through a long search for the face of Christ.

Prayer's purpose is not simply to refresh our strength, or to prevent our attention from being absorbed by limited, varied objectives. It is a question of collecting and ordering these objectives in relation to a love that pierces them and makes all our calculations relative. For "the reason to love God is God himself, and the measure of that love is to love him without measure."[9]

Christ in Us

One way of expressing the relationship between prayer and action places prayer at the center of life, taking hold of it and conforming it to the image of Christ. There is another, however, which places prayer as an open way to Christ, in order that he might vitalize all our life, in the sense described by Saint Paul: "It is no longer I who live, but Christ who lives in me" (Gal. 2:20).

This phrase from the Apostle is at the center of Christian mysticism; at the same time it is the key to a true presence in the world, to a life that seeks to be transparent to God. In that condition our existence, rather than shriveling inside itself in the illusion of

43

being something in its own right, is able to become an offering.

"You in me and I in you, Jesus my beloved, behold what I bring to you in the burnt-offering of prayer: I have nothing else. That which I am in you and which I see in you, I give entirely to you." This prayer of a medieval nun, Gertrude d'Helfta,[10] is one that every Christian would want to make his own.

In itself alone, action alternately elates us and makes us despair; it enriches us and devours us; it concentrates our energies and disperses them; it tends to give us too high an opinion of ourselves, then reduces us to self-contempt. Prayer can and must free us from all that, by offering our action to Christ as a sacrifice and the occasion for his life within us. Prayer restores our true relationship: we are nothing without Christ, but in him we are given inestimable value.

HUMAN ACTION, THE BODY OF PRAYER

Having outlined how prayer can and must be at the heart of action, we then ask if the opposite is also true. Is human action at the heart of prayer? Certainly we can defend the notion and show how prayer is woven into the warp and woof of our lives, and how what we experience on earth can, in some way, be recaptured and enveloped by prayer and thus be found at its center.

A Test of Authenticity

However, on careful examination it seems, rather, that human action is the *body* of prayer. By this I mean that it endows prayer with a weight, a reality, and a human density without which prayer would not be authentic. As I pointed out previously, we cannot claim that our action exists only to give body to our prayer; here I want to underscore the fact that prayer must be incorporated into what we are and into what we do in order for it to be *our* prayer: the prayer of men and women and not the prayer of angels playing fools.

In fact, the mark of human action on prayer attests, in a necessary way, that it is truly a human person who prays—a person who does not exist in the eyes of God except in his earthly and human responsibilities and relationships. Additionally, the mark of action on prayer attests, in a way no less necessary, that it is truly *God* to whom one prays; God in his love for the world and in his mysterious presence in history, the God of Jesus Christ in whom the promise of the Kingdom took an earthly, historic form in the life of a man.

Thus prayer can find in action an assurance of and a means to psychological health. It can be an antidote against the risk of prayer being the cry of that which in man is poorly integrated, fears others, runs away from responsibilities; against the additional danger of prayer being a cry addressed to a God who is only the product and image of man's infantile desires for power and security.

Exploring the world, tapping its energies, building the city of man, making history—all of these things are not accidental; they constitute man as God has created and called him. The earth and other persons, in a precise but limited way, are part of the life man has received from God.

So human tasks are necessary dimensions of the gift of self to God, in faith and prayer.

Prayer and Sanctification

"Not every one who says 'Lord, Lord,' shall enter the kingdom of heaven, but he who does the will of my Father who is in heaven" (Matt. 7:21). Detached from concrete obedience, prayer will only be words, "hot air." To pray is to respond to the word of God, but in order to receive that word, one must practice it, as the New Testament repeats over and over.

Prayer, therefore, demands not only faithfulness in the social and earthly dimensions of our life, but, through that faithfulness, a life that receives the Holy Spirit and seeks to be animated and shaped by him. The desire to see God, which is prayer, implies purity of heart (Matt. 5:8), in other words the desire without reserve to be God's.

"He who does what is true comes to the light" (John 3:21). If we understand "comes to the light" as the very movement of prayer in its attention to God, we shall also grasp how much our approach to the light depends on putting into practice the truth which we have already received from that light.

In his letter to the Colossians, Paul expressed the same thing when he indicated what he asked for them: that God would allow them to be filled "with the knowledge of his will in all spiritual wisdom and understanding"—in other words, the attention to God which constitutes prayer. The consequence: that they would "lead a life worthy of the Lord, fully pleasing to him"—prayer calling forth the human action that corresponds to it, but which is at the same time the condition of the deepening of prayer; "and increasing in the knowledge of God," animated by his energy. And the process repeats itself endlessly: prayer prolongs itself in human action, progress in the knowledge of God translates itself by "all endurance and patience with joy," and, in return, these qualities of action evoke a prayer of thanksgiving (Col. 1:9–12).

We see, in prayer, that transparency of attention is simultaneously the *seed* and the *fruit* of the sanctification of life—of thoughts, words, activities, and motives.

Sanctification—the term sounds odd today, perhaps because it has been understood in too negative a sense, a list of measures to guard against sin and to protect one from evil. But that defensive aspect of holiness is secondary. It makes sense only as a consequence of the primary aspect, which shines forth in the life of Christ. Holiness is first of all a radiance of love, coming from a commitment of the whole being. Sin does not consist only of doing evil; primarily it is failing to live resolutely the gift of love and thereby fleeing from the responsibilities and brotherhood of a man on earth—and, what is more, a man who understands the meaning of life as a calling of God.

If holiness is thought of as a struggle, conducted despite human commitments, it will rightly be suspected of leading to withdrawal. Neither does it suffice to say that holiness must be lived in all the dimensions of our human action. Rather, it must be said that this human action *itself* is to be lived as holiness, as the way to belong to God. To put it another way, the sanctification of a Christian does not take place anywhere other than in the midst of his commitments and his brotherhood with his neighbor—in his family, his work, his city, his Church. It is there that God awaits him, to walk with him.

Events and Prayer

In these various aspects, human action can appear as that which gives prayer its density, its weight, and its body. But there is more. In recent years it has often been recalled that God speaks to men and women through events. Not that events are added to the word of God as a new word, but that events challenge and send us back to that word so that we may rediscover its reality. If, therefore, in the world of men where we undertake our action, there occurs any event—the most particular or the most universal—that challenges us in this way, prayer is directly concerned. Events can become the fabric of prayer, the object of meditation, the motive for an appeal to God. In order to take on the value of signs, they must be scrutinized in faith and be received spiritually. For this reason our actions, and our involvements, large or small, give content and body to prayer.

The world and the events in which our actions involve us provide occasions for the joy or the concern of God. Prayer does not consist of trying to interest God in the life and history of men. He was interested long before we were! Rather, linked with our action, it consists of meeting God in events and trying to see in them the meaning they have for

48

God and the value that he first placed upon them.

* * * * *

This is enough to suggest that neither prayer nor human action is to be despised as such. Both have a place in the same life, the same person. But they do not simply replace one another. In this way they show the necessary but inconvenient fact that man is not one-dimensional.

Until the resurrection there will always be a certain tension between prayer and human action. The cause of that tension does not lie in prayer and that action. For a man to refuse to pray or to act would be to deny one of his dimensions. Yet obviously this profound and unstable reciprocity between prayer and action can only be affirmed in a life that recognizes God as its all. That is faith.

Yes, there is a necessary reciprocity between prayer and action. But perhaps it is important to point out here that in the life of an individual Christian action cannot and should not be forced to take the form of direct, specific political or social commitment. That would narrow the Christian presence in the world so as to exclude children, old people, the handicapped, and also all those whose personal gifts or circumstances orient them in another direction. Certainly one can say that in human existence everything is political, but this is true in a general sense, and this does not necessarily imply a specific commitment to organizing the city of man.

Now what about Christian men and women who join "contemplative" communities? Is that meaningful? And, more important, can it be justified? The organization of these persons' lives around and in terms of prayer presupposes a certain distance from the world and from society. Is this justified in light of what we have seen to be the relation between prayer and action in human unity?

No one person can achieve all of the dimensions of Christian vocation with intensity and absolute commitment. Each person emphasizes in his or her life an aspect of the gospel, so all Christians together have some chance to express its richness. However, I am not arguing here for specialization—some people praying in the place of others who are acting in their place. Prayer cannot be detached from human action for some individuals more than for others, nor can that action be separated from prayer. The special emphases of different vocations should not be juxtaposed according to specializations; rather, they must be joined together in a reciprocity whereby they receive their justification from each other. And that justification is like a sign or a parable: the absolute, whatever it may be, which I try to live with a certain emphasis within the obedience of my vocation, has a meaning for others; those others are thereby concretely related to it, even if they themselves must give it a lesser accent in their lives. But it is not for me to tell them the meaning of the parable. They must solve it for themselves. My role will be to discern the calls which their own emphases give to me, for they cannot be absent from my life, even if they must have less weight for me.

The life of a contemplative community, whether it wants it to be so or not, is unavoidably made up of human involvements, not only spiritual ones in the communion of the Church, but very material (and spiritual) ones in the place where the community is located. It is difficult to see any way in which it could neglect them. Nevertheless, such are not its essential goal or calling. If the monastic goal is no more than simple absence from the world, then the accent on prayer and the search for God loses its meaning. That relative absence from the world becomes significant for those who have eyes to see, because —and to the extent that—it is a paradoxical form of presence in the world. It is finally a political act and a sort of protest: a strong and decisive way of saying that the world and the way it is organized do not make sense in themselves and that the absolute, the Kingdom, which is the ultimate meaning of everything, is near. This is silent protest against the human tendency to become alienated in the nonessential, to become impassioned over the transient, to confuse the objectives of life on earth with the final and absolute goal. But it also involves a modest affirmation, full of hope, that the defeats which more or less radically mark all human enterprise can be offered as accepted poverty and, thus, as a waiting for God and a welcoming of his power.

This is surely a partial but primary aspect of the gospel. And it is a grace that certain persons emphasize this aspect in their lives. Moreover, they are able to do so because other Christians, in line with the incarnation, stress another aspect of the promise of the Kingdom for the world. But being such a sign of the Kingdom to come is not the *goal* of the contemplative communities and of their kind of life. It is only a *result*, a meaning that they take on in the eyes of those who interpret them in faith. The goal itself is free and humble—to seek God with an absolute desire, which implies a certain solitude, a silence, a concentration, and, therefore, a precise but limited emphasis. It is true that every person is limited, and one man cannot be at the oven and in the mill at the same time.

However, one should avoid accepting these limits too easily or settling into one's vocation with an easy conscience (in the pejorative sense of the term). In contemplative communities today many men and women question, sometimes anxiously, the legitimacy of their being set relatively apart, and of their alienation from the present political and technological world. Certainly there can be false distances and alienations to criticize and suppress. A given contemplative community may be able to find new forms for putting itself in better touch with its social milieu and in greater brotherhood with the poor. But in essentials, contemplatives would certainly be untrue to their own calling if they traded it for an active, traditional form of presence in the world. And, on the other hand, they would be unfaithful to their fellow men if they did not sense the limitations of their vocation.

Let them not simply pass from an easy conscience to a bad conscience! Neither let them try to justify

52

themselves. Rather, in concrete and explicit reciprocity, let them admire and rejoice in conjugal faith and social commitment wherever they observe them. Let them be able to receive these commitments, which are different from their own, into their spiritual attention and prayer, as something that also truly belongs to them. Let the contemplative communities be places where other Christians and all men who search will be welcome at the liturgy and in the quest for the essential: the face of God. In return, may these communities be justified and renewed in their own vocation, which is for others a parable of the coming Kingdom, limited but essential.

This is what the most lucid of "committed" Christians ask of them. Consider the beautiful and vibrant appeal made spontaneously by a Latin American woman, a student and political militant in 1970:

> Contemplatives! In the name of all humanity, of the continents which struggle for their full liberation; in the name of revolutionary politicians, of the peasant, worker, and student masses; in the name of men of science, of intellectuals, of artists, I beg you: Do not be afraid to live your vocation. Do not be ashamed to continue to live it intensely. Do not extinguish that light which you have discovered and which the world needs.
>
> If you do not know how to live your adventure completely, will you not cease to give precisely that which is up to you to offer to men and women? If you permit yourselves to become lukewarm and do not give yourselves entirely to your calling, coming even to doubt its significance, will you not be on the way to

killing something which you have been given to make grow? Sometimes, under the pretext of involvement with people, will you not be tempted to justify your lack of faith in a God who has always the right to be loved *gratuitously* today, as well as in all periods of history?

Contemplatives! In the name of all those who struggle known or anonymous, of all those who are engaged in the construction of a new society, I ask you urgently not to renounce your vocation. Know how to be completely attentive to people, in sharing their efforts all the way, their successes and failures, their struggles. Live in the rhythm of the sufferings and the joys of people. But do not be afraid to do it on the basis of your vocation. Seek new forms, to be sure, but do not reject the *essence* which you have received from the Lord. The world expects it of you, although it does not know it, although it does not say it.

Contemplatives! Do not let yourselves be guided by misleading evidence. Be faithful to God, faithful to men and women of today, by being faithful to the *heart* of your vocation.

LOVE OF GOD, LOVE OF MAN

The reciprocity of prayer and action is obviously closely linked to the relationship between love of God and love of neighbor. As that relationship is often questioned today, it calls for some reflections here.

One thinks first of all of that quotation from John, which has taken on new prominence today: "If anyone says, 'I love God,' and he hates his

54

brother, he is a liar; for he who does not love his brother whom he has seen, cannot love God whom he has not seen" (1 John 4:20).

Because of atheist critics, we are today in danger of isolating that verse and reducing the love of God to the love of neighbor. But two verses further on, John says, in a complementary sense: "By this we know that we love the children of God, when we love God and obey his commandments" (1 John 5:2).

In the past, it seems true that there was a tendency to reduce love of neighbor to love of God; that people frequently spoke of loving the neighbor "for God" as if that love passed through the neighbor without stopping there, without taking him seriously, without loving him personally. And it is certain that one sort of pietism, by opposing God to the world, was able to turn the attention of Christians away from people and their real lives. But without such attention there is no true love.

A reform was therefore necessary. But this reform must not end up at the same idea: that God and the world are competitors, mutually limiting each other, and that one must eliminate God or confuse him with humanity in order to be truly attentive to the neighbor. It was never because one loved God too much that he did not love his neighbor enough; rather, it was because he loved God too little, too poorly, and in a surreptitious seeking for self.

Love of God does not need to be based upon its earthly usefulness. In order for our love of man to demonstrate and even express our love for God, it is first necessary that this love of God be a true love, one that does not hold back or calculate. It must be a love that addresses itself to God himself and for him, one that establishes itself solely on the incommensurable and prior love of God for us.

In the human experience, with its psychological roots and long personal history, it is our relationship to other persons that permits us to arrive at a relationship with God. In that respect, we must say that during all our lives we move from the love of men and women to the love of God.

But more profoundly, at the level of experienced faith, the opposite must also happen. Spiritually we move from the love of God to the love of neighbor. The love of men is the route necessary to arrive at communion with God, but this is so because God is mysteriously present in each exchange of true love between two human persons.

So if love for God is not primary in us, if it does not aim at expressing itself through our entire lives, if it is not total, if it does not find its meaning in itself, then it is not God whom we love, the God from whom we receive ourselves, by whom we are, without whom we are nothing. Once we glimpse who God is, in what he disclosed to us between Christmas and Pentecost, once we glimpse that he is named Love and that he is pure love, we can only love him for himself. And that love appears as the very meaning and opportunity of our lives.

When viewed as a movement of man, love may seem somewhat the same whether aimed at God or neighbor. However, God and neighbor are not on the same plane, nor do they limit each other reciprocally. That is why we are not reduced to trying to divide our love between God and man, as if what is given to one is taken away from the other. In fact, as Dietrich Bonhoeffer pointed out, using a musical analogy, it is precisely the opposite that must happen. In order for our ties of love on earth to unfold in a rich and free polyphony, it is all the more necessary that our lives ring loudly with the fundamental theme, the *cantus firmus:* God and his eternity, loved by us completely. It is around this main theme and based upon it that the counterpoint is harmonized, distinct but inseparable from it.[11]

Love of God: Foundation, Dynamism, and Horizon

From the viewpoint of a person who confesses that Christ is the Lord of his life, it is the love of God that is the foundation of the love of neighbor, and not the other way around. But the love of God undergirds and expressly calls forth the love of neighbor.

How is it founded? Briefly, in the love of God we attain both our truth and the truth of the neighbor and, therefore, the truth of human love. For the truth of humanity is to be and to know ourselves to be the objects of God's love. How can I hope to truly love my neighbor? To put it otherwise, how can I hope that it is truly I who love and not the doubting forces within me, mixed with egoism and self-interest? How, if not by approaching my truth, which is to know myself to be loved by God, and by responding to that love?

And how can I hope to truly love my neighbor as he really is—not according to the appearance he gives himself or according to the image that I prefer to make of him? How, if not by discovering that my neighbor is someone irreplaceable in the heart of God, that God loves him infinitely, and that I, myself, cannot do otherwise than participate in that love of God for him.

So the love of God within us is the source of our love of neighbor. But it is also its *enveloping dynamism*. A true relationship of love between two persons can be found only through the love of God—to be precise, in the person of Christ. As Bonhoeffer has noted, there is no direct spiritual communion between two human beings: Christ is the mediator.[12] To put it precisely, he is mediator not as a third party or as an intermediary, but as one who unites us to our neighbor because he has entered into an inner unity with each of us, with me who knows it, and with my neighbor who perhaps is not aware of it.

There is more. If the love of God is the source and the dynamism of our love of neighbor, it is also *the pole and the horizon*. To be sure, today we underline the necessity of loving the other gratuitously for himself, without the hidden motive of converting him, if that were to mean pressure or a goal in itself. To love truly is to will the good of the other without pretending to know ahead of time in detail what that good is—and especially without wishing to impose it. The truth of love implies humility and gratuitousness.

But our love would cease to be authentic if we had to renounce the assurance that ultimately God is the good of our neighbor, as of ourselves. Love would degrade itself into complicity if it did not tend toward God, explicitly or silently, according to the situation.

But what about the love evidenced by non-Christians, which is often so great and profound? It certainly exists. But since some people love without reference to the gospel, either the gospel has nothing to say to us about love or all true love, explicitly or not, is evangelical—that is, founded, enveloped, and polarized by the love of God. God alone is the judge of hearts, so we move beyond our competence and abilities when we seek to make comparisons in this realm; we either presume to know the intentions on which other people base their love, or we claim that a given person loves apart from God.

God in the Neighbor, the Neighbor in God

It is not false to say, with a certain Christian humanism, that I love God in loving the person of my neighbor; neither is it false to say, with a certain pietism, that I must love my neighbor in God and for God. The two formulas become debatable only when they presuppose a rivalry between God and the neighbor, when they tend to subjugate one to the other as if God and man were located on the same level and limited each other reciprocally.

Even in a human perspective such a thing would be inconceivable. Can you imagine a conjugal love in which one of the partners said to the other: "I have no time for you. I will love you through the person of my colleagues or my neighbors?" No, it is through loving your partner for himself or herself, with all the time and attention necessary, that you also learn to love other persons as concrete human beings.

Analogically, if I judge it to be a waste of time to love God for himself, then to that extent the person of my neighbor is erased from my concern and becomes merely an idea. Conversely, if my neighbor is but a pretext for or a means of loving God, it is no longer God whom I love, but an abstraction—or myself by substitution.

Let's try to be precise. These two loves preserve each other mutually: the first founded on the truth of the second, and the second attesting to the truth of the first. Our love for men psychologically measures the *human authenticity* of our love for God, keeping it from becoming empty words or an escape from reality. And our love for God measures the *spiritual quality,* the depth of the roots and the continually renewed openness, of our love for neighbor. It keeps us from reducing the neighbor to a thing, or from making him or her an idealized absolute. It holds our relationship to the neighbor open to something beyond, to an infinite beyond.

We must remain more or less in tension between these two loves, and that tension corresponds to our limits, which we must accept without partiality. Our attention always goes back and forth between God and neighbor. The difficulty is subjective, and we must not transform it into an opposition in principle.

To an extent, we are always gathering together the pieces of ourselves. We experience things successively, in fragments, and that wearies and disappoints us. It is through faith that the real unity of our relationship to God and our relationship to neighbor appears. It is in faith, experienced as prayer and as love, that the encounter between prayer and love appears to us in its fruitfulness.

Patriarch Athanagoras said:

> Love nourishes prayer and prayer nourishes love. To intercede and to give thanks is to permit the blood of the chalice to irrigate the universe. "In all things, give thanks," wrote the Apostle. Be amazed that God exists; then you will discover that everything is alive. Prayer becomes existence, the existence of one who ceases to be closed in upon himself and who opens to that which is immense and simple. The pure in heart shall see God and the meek shall inherit the earth.[13]

And Paul Tillich wrote: Religion is first of all an open hand to accept a gift, and only in the second place is an active hand to distribute gifts.[14]

Appendix: A Hard Question for Many— the Meaning of Work and Prayer

For many Christians today, the impression that prayer has become something artificial in their lives is only one of the symptoms of a general malaise about their work and its place in the general economy.

In the old days, it seems, men didn't have the same expectation of fulfilling themselves in work. Perhaps they had a more pessimistic view of their pilgrimage on earth; in any case, they lived with less demanding subjectivity. They were readier to be content with little; when necessary they accepted it with resignation. But today's mentality, having imbibed the idea of progress and greatly admiring technological and economic success, appears very optimistic, even in its criticism and rebellion. It is speechless whenever it runs into the deep-seated ambiguity of all projects, of all accomplishments, and of all progress. Defeat can only be an accident, an error, or an injustice.

Efficient and triumphalist, this mentality is consequently badly prepared to accept anything that would limit the earthly fulfillment of persons or create any obstacles to happiness. The very idea of accepting limitations is suspect as an escape into resignation and passivity. Once the means to accomplish something have been provided, the result must follow automatically, as if the life of a person and of mankind simply proceeds from the laws of technology.

These remarks are not meant to be critical; they are simply an effort to understand why in our time, in "developed" countries, a thoroughly optimistic mentality and a very demanding subjectivity can only react dramatically when they collide with each other.

* * * * *

This is certainly what has happened to many people today. For some, meaninglessness appears in the very purpose of their work, or in the conditions of their work. For others, who have more interesting jobs, meaninglessness appears in the way their work is related to the economy as a whole. It is no longer just the fragmenting of work on the assembly line that is to blame. Many skilled workers, even managers of industry and commerce, see themselves trapped inside a sort of immense machine that pulverizes them by turning in upon itself.

A person must be able to expect from his or her work not only a way to earn a living, but some meaning that it takes on by sharing in a brotherhood of service. For the Christian, it is in this sense that his work—all work—appears as a sharing in the growth of the Kingdom.

So what happens if, instead of mutual service to meet human needs, the mobilization of technology and men for work has no purpose beyond itself? What happens if the object of a business enterprise ends up being no more than keeping up to date and grabbing its share of the market?

This impression of meaninglessness weighs particularly upon the individuals whose responsibilities for business management command their time, energies, and attention in such a way as to upset their personal and family lives. One hesitates to pay such a high human price even when the goal seems worthy, but when it is a race toward meaninglessness—what then? The less these individuals look into themselves, the more they escape this malaise. And since prayer implies some rediscovery of self, it is apparent why it becomes problematic under these conditions.

Curiously, as so much work becomes its own goal and often uselessly engenders more of itself, this impression of meaninglessness reaches the people who appear to be the most positive and assured members of our society: the engineers, the businessmen, the industrialists. And this is happening just at the moment when theology and the preaching of the Church, ashamed of a past that neglected earthly values and the work of men and women, are coming out with views full of optimism. But now the Church is encountering people who often judge her views as unrealistic and utopian, people who are disappointed, pessimistic, and sometimes bewildered to the very degree that they are most representative of the optimistic mentality.

This is not the place to propose economic or technical solutions. It is the spiritual dimension of the question that catches my attention. Moreover, my dialogue with some of these restless individuals makes me think that those who do not simply wish to drop out of the struggle or to scuttle their business have extremely limited room for maneuvering, for slowing the race toward meaninglessness while still remaining competitive. The problem is serious enough when it concerns only the individual and his family; it becomes extremely complex for persons responsible for a large number of employees. One can only hope for a change in mentality great enough to permit vast sectors of society to restore technology to its proper place and to rediscover a goal that has a human meaning, an economy based on real needs.

It is not enough to say that a business at least has meaning in providing a livelihood for its employees. It must appear as a service to its clients.

* * * * *

Thus there is a strong and frequent impression of meaninglessness in work and in human involvement, where service must give way to competition and usefulness to rivalry. And this impression is experienced as a weighty obstacle to prayer. Why? Because, in the last analysis, prayer reveals that meaninglessness and begins to make it unbearable.

We are back at the profound interrelationship between prayer and action, but here it appears from a negative angle. Deprived of its meaning in men's eyes, life cannot relate to God, and prayer is ejected from life. Man tries to escape in action.

First of all, however, let us ask if it is really true that the impression of the meaninglessness of work extends through all life. Certainly the worry, the expenditure of energy, and the burden of responsibility seem objectively to be like tentacles squeezing a man's whole life. But, at the same time, the meaning of existence is not simply to be identified with work.

It is necessary then to ask if the impression of meaninglessness in work, which some people feel, isn't exaggerated. Except for the manufacture and sale of materials that are clearly injurious or totally useless, the service of mankind remains present in all work, even if that service is unfortunately relegated to the background by major emphasis on competition and specialization.

This is not said as cheap consolation, nor as an excuse for passively making the best of a bad situation. Nevertheless, the economy of which one is a part can be subject to very serious criticism, can even be unacceptable, without being totally devoid of any service to mankind. One can oppose the meaninglessness while simultaneously acknowledging that it is not a question of total meaninglessness. The absolute, even in meaninglessness, is rarely attained.

The two questions seem to dominate the spiritual aspect of the problem. There is no need to consider prayer as something alien to one's existence, so long as one is able to discern utility—and therefore at least as partial service—in his work, and so long as one's entire life is not claimed by the dimension of work.

Certainly we do not want prayer just to fill up the gaps of our lives—the defeats, the meaninglessness, the weaknesses. We do not want prayer to be born of our powerlessness. On the other hand, we must not think naively that prayer springs forth only in a life that is humanly successful and esteems itself fulfilled. All that we are, including the defeats and pains of life, consititutes the body of our prayer. Prayer is able to give meaning to that which seems meaningless. We must often face and endure tension between prayer and the conditions of our action. We continually search for the unity and meaning of life. We do not make the tensions that exist within us into a problem of principle, into a supposed incompatibility between *prayer* and *action*. We believe in their profound and essential unity, and this faith establishes our patient and ardent search for harmony between them.

To the extent that the spiritual life is able to make itself even more intense in the face of unsatisfactory working conditions, it can bear fruit even on the level of work. As an inspiration, as a source of patience and tenacity, as a demand for meaning, will not prayer play its own role in searching for and creating an economic and social life in which production is at the service of people?

NOTES

1. On this subject, see Fons d'Hoogh, "Prayer in a Secularized Society," Concilium 49: *Secularization and Spirituality,* pp. 37–51.

2. John A.T. Robinson is Anglican bishop of Woolwich and author of *Honest to God* (Philadelphia: Westminster, 1963).

3. Paul Claudel, *Toi, qui es-tu?*

4. Dietrich Bonhoeffer, *Ethics,* trans. Neville Horton Smith; ed. Eberhard Bethge (New York: Macmillan Paperback Edition, 1965), p. 189.

5. Robert Oppenheimer, "Perspectives sur les arts et les sciences," cited in *Signes des temps* (1967, no. 3), p. 18.

6. Gaston Berger, *L'Homme moderne et son éducation* (Paris 1962), p. 195.

7. On this subject, see B. de Margerie, "Le Christ, la sécularisation et la consécration du monde," *Nouvelle Revue Théologique* 91 (April 1968) 370–395.

8. Bernard, *On Consideration,* I, II, 3.

9. *Ibid, Treatise on the Love of God,* I.

10. Gertrude d'Helfta, *Exercises,* VI.

11. Dietrich Bonhoeffer, *Résistance et soumission* (Geneva 1967), p. 130.

12. *Ibid., Life Together,* trans. John W. Doberstein (New York: Harper, 1954), p. 21.

13. See O. Clement, *Dialogues avec le Patriarche Athénagoras* (Paris: 1969), p. 182.

14. Paul Tillich, *La dimension oubliée* (Paris 1969), p. 72.

3

The unspoken prayer of the Lord's poor

Be Satisfied with Little?

In principle, prayer has its place at the center of life and action (as shown in Chapter 2), at the heart of the life and action of a man who understands himself completely as an élan toward being, a calling of God (as seen in Chapter 1). However, there is often a very great distance between that principle and the place that prayer actually has in our existence.

As a norm, the day should be ordered around prayer and enter into its movement. In fact, the day is more often already crammed full. So one tries to reserve a moment (or two) for prayer during a day already complete in itself, much as one hammers a wedge into a log.

Realistically, one must be resigned to this situation. But one must at least recognize that the correct order of priorities has thereby been reversed and that, therefore, in the long run, prayer runs a good chance of seeming to be stuck onto life like a bothersome appendage, a foreign body, a parenthesis, an aside.

And there are other drawbacks. Prayer suffers from being wedged into a period of time surrounded by urgent activities. It is necessary to get started quickly, but rarely can we leap wholeheartedly into prayer. Ordinarily we can begin only slowly, taking time to collect ourselves. Without such recollection prayer seems external to us and our existence, because we do not know how or are not able to enter into prayer.

That is not all. Reserving time for prayer under such conditions requires a real effort of will and discipline, which excessively and dangerously accentuates the task and the duty that prayer represents. This becomes a detriment to its grace and joy—a joy that is never easy.

We can put up with these conditions some of the time, counting on the grace of God and telling ourselves that God blesses our intentions to pray even if we have not been able to adapt ourselves deeply to those intentions. But it is not difficult to predict —and to observe—that our very understanding of prayer is going to be distorted if this continues for weeks, months, years. Prayer will be carried as a burden. It will tend to become mere words that no longer truly express our feelings.

That same thing is true of liturgical prayer, for the same reasons. We blame the words, saying they are old and worn out, which is sometimes true. But that is not the fundamental problem. The form and expression of common prayer and of the prayer of the Christian alone in his room or praying with his spouse all seem old fashioned and formal even before they are spoken, if we remain outside that form and those expressions, or if we have the illusion that they will enable us to pray despite ourselves.

Whether I try to play the violin, learn Russian, learn to ski or take photographs—not to mention trying to keep up to date in my work—nothing important in my existence can interest me, give me pleasure, or show progress in five-minute spurts every week or so or in a few days out of the year.

Whether I try to write an article or an important letter, resolve a problem, discuss something with spouse or friend, or even listen to a quartet or do a crossword puzzle, nothing creative is possible without taking enough time to enter into it and to get underway.

Do I want to pray in the same way I scan magazines, glance at the barometer, light a cigarette, or start the motor of a car?

I know very well what has to happen in me when I try to accomplish something that challenges my laziness or my inveterate interest in self. It takes some mobilization of energy, a little courage, a decided effort, a pulling of self out of lethargy, a way of cutting short the impulse to yawn, stretch, and mutter "so what," a way of ignoring all the other things I could obviously be doing in that instant.

And since we all know this about ourselves, would we want it to be different in the case of prayer? Is our faith so poor as to confuse freedom and spontaneity in the case of prayer? Do we say prayer is irrelevant to life? Certainly, if for us life, and in particular our inner life, means passive consumption. For prayer, it will not suffice to drop a coin into the slot and pull the handle. It is not enough to push a button.

Obviously the tempo of modern life does not facilitate the setting aside of moments for concentration and creativity. But, especially for prayer, the true obstacle is not the rhythm of today's civilizaton, but the multiplied facilities for escaping ourselves in the distractions, superficiality, noise, and pictures that whirl around our eyes and ears. Is not Christian asceticism, which we can never discount entirely, to be lived today precisely in this environment as an apprenticeship of freedom—the freedom to become and to remain ourselves?

Then What to Do?

So first we must ask seriously if we do not need to make choices, perhaps excruciating choices. Perhaps we need to trim our activities in order to set aside more than such a little bit of time that prayer cannot live and grow in us, leaving us disappointed if not disgusted with it.

Next we must try to train ourselves to set aside in each day brief relays of prayer, a few seconds during the very numerous gaps in our schedules and movements, to think of God and to think of ourselves before him, in order to restore the essential trajectory of our existence.

But we must honestly recognize that this will not be enough. For those "flashes" to be possible, and for the words of our prayer—with a group, in the family, or alone—to maintain their density during the time we explicitly set aside for it, we need something else. We need moments for what I call *contemplation*. For some people once a day, for others once a week.

We need free time, a rather long time (half an hour? an hour?), during which we are disengaged from the bustle, during which we risk, if necessary, being bored. We need a time that is truly empty if God does not fill it, one we do not hasten to fill ourselves or to escape from soon on any pretext. We need a time during which our prayer is able to go as far as it can, a time that has but one purpose—to express our thirst for God, and primarily to let that thirst deepen in us and appear as that which most radically makes us what we are.

It is not a question of a "retreat"—that remains occasional. Neither is it an exercise to be added on to daily prayer or to the liturgy as something entirely different.

To speak of "time" for contemplation, even to suggest that a specific length of time should be required, is not without danger. There is a risk of getting discouraged in advance. Yet in this matter we must be able to be serious and audacious in our proposals, while simultaneously not scorning or minimizing the little that we are doing now. There is also the objection that the quality of prayer has nothing to do with its length. That is true. God is not subject to time. But we are, irremediably so! And it would be naive or somewhat dishonest to deny that length of time matters in our attention to God, in the generosity (or stinginess) which our prayer expresses, in the movement by which our persons seek to pull themselves together.

73

Contemplation?

What does the term "contemplation" mean? As I use it here, it does not refer to a special kind of prayer, but rather to that which underlies all true prayer, whether said with others or alone with God. It is an inner silence in which the words of prayer resound and come to life; it is a primary, fundamental attitude within which prayer's expressions are born. Contemplation is a presence of self before God, a spiritual attention that prolongs and carries the prayed word as much as it is carried by it. But to remain as the underlying resource of prayer, contemplation, thus understood, must also have certain moments to be experienced *in itself.*

One might compare it to the need one feels in human relationships. Habitual conversation of a couple or a community, meetings of a work or study team, consultations with friends or colleagues, all generally have a rather well-defined goal, whether it be seeking to clarify a question, making a point, planning for the future, laying the groundwork for a project, or working together. In and through such diverse encounters there is certainly a reciprocal personal presence, a relationship of friendship or of love. But it is good and necessary that this interpersonal presence and face-to-face relationship also be able to express itself sometimes without any other goal than itself, in a more gratuitous, more free, and more intimate way.

And if one has truly attained the intimacy of love or the intensity of friendship, one knows very well that words and sentences become less important in terms of their precise content (one no longer discusses), while they become more important, more rare, and more precious in terms of the whole background they evoke.

By analogy, it is the same for contemplation, which underlies all true prayer but also is experienced in itself at certain times.

Therefore, in this sense, all that one can say about prayer also applies to contemplation and vice versa; nevertheless, there is a difference in emphasis. Beyond all organized formulations, contemplation tends to become, through awkward groping, that "free look, penetrating, immobile" as Hugh of Saint Victor defined it. It seeks to be a silent attention to God, to his will, to his presence in us and in the world. Which is not to say that it rejects words and thoughts, but it covers them with silence, meditates on them, and tends to depend on only a few words, a single theme.

The following pages attempt to suggest what contemplation is, taking the view of a poor and modest attitude on man's part, but a grand and mysterious reality on God's part. I will not speak of methods of contemplation, or at least only very indirectly. One begins as one can, according to who one is and especially in relation to what one seeks.

As an analogue, a man does not learn from a book in advance how to encounter his fiancée. This does not mean that, in each encounter, he will not draw on his widest human experience nor, more specifically, on what he learns about himself and his fiancée in the course of their encounters.

Very simply and mysteriously contemplation

tries to love God by the most attentive presence possible to God's presence. The point of departure is in remembering God, in recalling to whom one responds and whom one seeks—God as he reveals himself in his work and Spirit and as he has manifested his presence in the history of his people and in the course of one's life. It is a question of remembering his mighty deeds in the past (Ps. 77:12) in order to enter into his present and to open oneself to his future.

This memory of faith works for some persons through self-examination, for others through meditation on a biblical passage, or through the slow recitation of a psalm or several verses of some other book of Scripture. Some are also helped by reading a few pages from a spiritual book or by considering an event just experienced or read about in a newspaper.

The rest is a matter of readiness, docility to grace, patience. Our personal sensibilities, our inner rhythms are, from the start, the "given" that God infinitely respects. Therefore, we do not have to force them or to twist them by seeking to follow the method of some other Christian in a servile way. On the contrary, it is more effective to give contemplation a personal tone and to live our own freedom within it. Subjectivism, then? No, for personal freedom lived before God seeks to be purified of all self-satisfaction.

In a sense, silent prayer by definition does not program itself. It is an adventure, like the pilgrimage of the children of Israel through the desert. That does not imply any negligence on our part. We must always question the truth of our contemplation, but never its value—for that would require us to take the place of God.[1]

"What are the conditions to pray well in silence? First one must be humble; second, have great hope; and third, one must be grafted onto Jesus Christ crucified."[2] That is what Saint Francis of Sales preached.

And this is what a present-day nun writes:

> In silent prayer it is necessary to expect all, and at the same time to expect nothing. To expect everything because "all things are possible to him who believes," (Mark 9:23) and especially to him who prays. And to expect nothing, knowing (and finding in this fact a blessing) that in any case one will not be rewarded visibly by God. It is marvelous to know that such gratuitousness is given to poor and undeserving folk such as we are. Paradoxically, the less one is rewarded, the more one is filled. I do not wish to employ excessive language when it concerns pure prayer. All must be experienced in the joyous simplicity of the children of God, and I am convinced that nothing inhuman can bear the divine seal.[3]

To Seek and to Find

How can one stimulate contemplation except with a few hints? It is related to the mystery of God itself and the mystery of our communion with God. One can approach it only by groping in apparently contradictory ways, which are actually dialectical, by first one tack and then another.

This is because God is in the most intimate part of our being and yet is always far beyond our outstretched hands. He is presence, but we are never able to hold him. He is absence by the excess of presence and of nearness. And contemplation is both seeking and finding *in one and the same movement*. Saint Augustine said that one seeks God because one has already found him: "One seeks him to find him with greater pleasure, and one finds him in order to seek him with more ardor."[4]

Not that God plays hide-and-seek with us. But his "holiness"—the infinite intensity of his presence and of his love, beyond all glory that we can understand, and the "timidity" of his love, this side of all distance and of all humility—escapes our grasp.[5]

God cannot be measured on our scale. But, in our immense thirst for being, we ourselves are not up to our own measure either. Everything becomes tiresome, everything but God, for he is simply beyond our measure, like an unfathomable abyss, yet simultaneously like the sun, an intensity of love that is ardent and sweet.

It is really enough to make us laugh and cry at the same time. It is enough to terrify us, to give us a single idea—forgetting it all in atheism or in a nice little superficial and reassuring religion. At the same time there is something within us that does not want to retreat. For we are not looking at that immense mystery from outside. It envelopes us, like an infinite and secret friendship. It comes to us like a call, and then it seems to move on ahead so that we press on, responding to that call. "Not that I have already obtained this or am already perfect; but I press on to make it my own, because Christ Jesus has made me his own" (Phil. 3:12).

All our fears, our terrors can then converge and transform themselves into the one legitimate fear,

78

which is an anxiety of love, a suffering for not loving God enough, for not opening ourselves sufficiently to the royal freedom he wishes to share with us so that we may share it with him. It is no longer a question of acting out of fear, but of fearing through love, as Dorotheus of Gaza said.[6] And what about contemplation at the heart of prayer? It is, first of all, an attention to and a consciousness of all that, a concentration on the essential that causes us to say to God with the psalmist: "Unite my heart to fear thy name" (Ps. 8:11). On some days it will prove to be a prolonged effort to center ourselves, a struggle against distractions and the desire to do other things. But even with the dispersion and the distractions, this struggle is a painful but blessed way of experiencing the fact that if we no longer belong to God it is primarily because we no longer belong to ourselves.

Let us not belittle this pain of being so miserable on certain days. May it become for us the concrete sign of a completely radical misery. For the power with which we feel it is the very measure of our openness to the presence of God. "Never forget that we are only wayfarers here, far from the homeland, driven forth from our inheritance. For he who does not know his desolation will lack the power to recognize his consolation," said Saint Bernard.[7] And Claudel has said, more concisely, "Only exile teaches one about the homeland."[8]

There are even days when we can only drag our inner selves along, nevertheless before God, in contemplation that seems to be pure tedium. God is there, but we, weighed down by ourselves, can only say with the psalmist: "I was like a beast before thee" (Ps. 73:22), deaf, blind, stupid before the delicacy of God. Is such contemplation a defeat? Only God can judge. But we live such days waiting for God, and from our point of view that is better than nothing.

For, as Saint Bernard wrote at the very end of his life: "It is a great good to seek God. I think that among all the blessings of the soul there is none greater than this. It is first among the gifts of God and the last resting place."[9] And the same author wrote to the pope: "There is only God that one can never seek in vain, even when one cannot find him."[10]

There is, therefore, a struggle, a slow mobilization of all our being, for, as Saint Caesarius wrote: "How can God be in your midst if you yourself are not there? It is not fitting for the priest to be absent from the temple of God."[11]

But at the same time there is rest, waiting, in which we seek less to make Christ enter than to let in him who stands at the door and knocks (Rev. 3:20), and to let him light the fire. The fuel for that fire —in the form of memories, concerns, and preoccupations—is the presence in us of human and Christian commitments. The flame is the love of Christ. Contemplation is not an escape from real life, it is a setting fire to life. Contemplation is neither an effort to empty self (as is sometimes said) nor to abstract the self from daily life. Of course, it implies a certain withdrawal and the firm desire to quiet the inner noises. Its movement, however, does not consist in chasing thoughts but rather in putting them in place, organizing them, and offering them to the fire of Christ.

To Receive and to Give

To seek and to find together describe contemplation. It is the same for two other terms: to receive and to give.

These two verbs, which seem opposed to each other in the experience of daily life, are joined and unified before God. Contemplation is not an exaltation of self. On the contrary, the presence of God makes us take note of our radical poverty, our essential dependence. "What have you that you did not receive?" (1 Cor. 4:7), beginning with your life, your person, all that you are. And in a lyric fashion, Philaretus of Moscow wrote: "Creatures are poised on the Word of God as on the point of a diamond, under the abyss of the divine infinite, above the abyss of their own nothingness."[12]

This effacement of self, this opening of hands to receive instead of closing them upon a possession, this renouncing of ownership is for us the very sign of the presence of God. "When we no longer find self within our hearts, it is because God is present there."[13]

And our offering consists of this: waiting. According to Lefebvre's very profound remark, "With God, to offer oneself is to offer oneself to his gifts."[14] To live for him is to live by him, as the entire life of Jesus testifies. To give thanks (*rendre grâce*) is to receive grace by recognizing that it comes from

God; it is the only way to receive it, for grace is not a thing but a communion.

The impression, which we can often have, of the absence of God is, for the most part, bound to the fact that spontaneously—almost necessarily—we think of God's presence in terms of having something. We wish to hold, to feel, and to possess. Our hands close on an emptiness because the presence of God must be understood and experienced in terms of being—more precisely, as a being-with, as a mutual gift. Is it God who absents himself, or is it we who remain reticent and limited in our will to be entirely with him and of him?

Contemplation is not a goal in itself; its quality and its success are beyond our appreciation. The days during which we experience only a bitter powerlessness to hold ourselves in dignity before God can often be the days when our contemplation is most authentic, if we offer that powerlessness as an appeal and as confidence.

Is this saying that contemplation neither can or should produce a living joy or even a warm enthusiasm in us? No, but those are neither its condition nor proofs of its authenticity. Those are graces, which are added and which must not be sought for themselves. In contrast to the more hidden and secret joy that is inherent in contemplation but is almost beyond the limits of our perception, these lively and warm graces are partially dependent on the sensitivity of the individual. And our sensitivity is not yet resurrected nor yet truly in harmony with the presence of God. It is still marked by our limitations and by the dark and cold areas inside us.

As we have seen, the words of our prayers and those of the prayers of the Church run the almost constant danger of seeming to be worn out. Even Scripture, as a result of rereading, can seem tiresome to us. Contemplation therefore has the task of bringing to life the words of the Bible and those of prayer, in all their depth and their transcendence.

Their depth: In the use our intellect makes of them, words tend to become abstract signs, to be dried up, and to be emptied of their savor. This is especially true of terms such as *salvation, grace, redemption*. Abstraction is even a function of the frequency with which these words are used. This abstraction is even a good thing because it allows us to think more rapidly. But the resulting danger is that words, especially the words of faith and prayer, tend to slide past without surprising us and without concretely expressing our reality. The words, all words, tend to become flat, to shrink, often to shrivel into a single meaning, like dried fruit, which must be soaked before eating.

Meditation is, therefore, necessary in order to "soak" the words of prayer in their original image so as to rediscover their connotations, to restore their vitality, and to unfold their richness of harmony. This puts into operation, on one hand, our Christian experience, the reference of everything to the living light of Christ and, on the other hand, our sensibilities, our poetic sense, our need for symbols, which come from the fact that we are inseparably both body and spirit.

Necessarily a prolongation of verbal prayer, contemplation is opposed to routine and laziness of spirit; it is also opposed to excesses of abstraction. It is a concern to deepen the words and sentences of the Bible, the language of the liturgy, and doctrinal formulations of the faith. Contemplation seeks to let them vibrate in the depth of our being, in a movement toward personal appropriation.

It would be completely unrealistic to wish to do without words, and entirely utopian to believe we can endlessly replace them with others that are more up-to-date. All the specific words of the Christian faith have a use in modern secular language. Without words—and without words adequately chosen and often refashioned by their biblical and Christian usage—our faith could not think or speak; it would evaporate. Naturally, faith also renews its vocabulary, but with the intelligence of a good disciple of the Kingdom, "who brings out of his treasure what is new and what is old" (Matt. 13:52).

Faith will never be able to do without adequately chosen words, and our love for God would be neither serious nor true if it tried to avoid the knowledge that results from our attention to the Word by which God makes himself known to us.

But let's be precise: contemplation—and meditation as part of contemplation—consists of constantly passing from knowledge to understanding, from the depth of words to transcendence of them. As Saint Ignatius of Antioch said: To possess in truth the word of Jesus is to be able "also to hear his silence."[15] For the words and the formulas of our faith are not points of arrival; like road signs they point the gaze of faith in the direction of goals they never reach.

*　*　*　*　*

One thinks for example of the word "heaven." "Our Father who art in heaven." Hasn't the term almost become unusable for anyone who is even vaguely aware of modern science? But people did not wait until the second half of the twentieth century to realize that, in Christian terminology, "heaven" is not the physical location of God. Passages in the writings of the Church Fathers show that even in their day the heaven of God was understood in terms of an inner attitude of man. Still, it is important that the word evoke something real for us, something of which we have understanding and experience. The import is not primarily scientific, but poetic: an immense space above us where birds and airplanes fly, where clouds race by, where the light comes from. With this connotation, the word "heaven" resounds as a symbol that is primarily human, and a symbol too important to be replaced.

In effect, whether or not the world is round, whether or not space is curved, changes nothing in the structure of our existential space.[16] Man stands with his head above his feet, the earth under his feet, and the sky over his head. The polarity of high and low is profoundly bound up with the way we experience and express good and bad, freedom and slavery, weight and weightlessness. Necessarily we have a graduated scale of values, and even the term "graduated" implies vertical movement from down to up. That vertical image, in tension with the horizontal line from past to future (as illustrated by the word "projection"), has become integral to the most basic and intimate realities that constitute our being and our life.

Thus heaven symbolizes the ultimate horizon of man's existence, its transcendence, the kind of space and dimensions that do not belong to man but toward which man is headed, because he comes from the earth yet cannot limit himself to it. The meaning of man is expressed to the degree that the physical reality designated by the term "heaven" refers to another sort of reality, one that man is able to experience and to speak of only by analogy with exterior, physical reality.

This is a human symbol of great density, which evokes a luminous transparency, a joyful lightness, a freedom without limits, an infinite value. We use this symbol because faith does not operate by abstraction, by removing the flesh from images. On the contrary, words are useful to faith to the extent of their richness in imaginative and sensitive connotations. But faith is not locked up in words and faith must take particular care to remember that its terminology has several levels. Unlike science, faith does not speak a language whose terms have only one possible meaning. Its language is symbolic. Its words have a fragile equilibrium, their meaning suggesting the indescribable density of reality, rather than enclosing and defining their object.

Faith does not hide itself in the words it uses. They serve, rather, as a point of leverage, projecting the spirit in an élan that aims at what lies beyond words.

It is, finally, very simple. It suffices that the word "heaven" becomes a word of love addressed to God, so that this word, far from imprisoning the spirit, transfigures itself and opens out like a wing. It is much the same in the languague of human love. Strictly speaking, that language is senseless and inadequate; it always says too much or too little. But it is only in precise terminology that love is unable to s⁻y anything. Its language is analogical and symbolic. No one is fooled, so long as the persons speaking it are tuned to the expression and understanding of such language, a language of mutual confidence and of reciprocal wonder.

*　*　*　*　*

The movement through words toward what is beyond words, the conversion of theological knowledge into spiritual knowledge, corresponds to a remark of Karl Barth: "True and proper language concerning God will always be a response to God, which overtly or covertly, explicitly or implicitly, thinks and speaks of God exclusively in the second person."[17]

Dionysius the Areopagite (a Greek theologian of the early centuries, whose works we have, but about whom we know nothing except his name) wrote: Certainly our knowledge of God begins "from the order that we discover in all beings . . . . [However] God is not part of that which is, and one is not able to know him through anything that exists, although he is All in All . . . . The way to know God which is most worthy of him is to know him by means of not-knowing . . . when intelligence, first detached from all beings, then going out from itself, is united in rays brighter than light."[18] In another work Dionysius explains: "The Author of all things places himself beyond all things."[19]

Molinié says, paradoxically, that in contemplation one meditates not so much to understand as to dissipate the illusion of having understood.[20]

This must not drive us to agnosticism, in which one no longer affirms nor denies anything. Neither should it make us think that it doesn't matter how we speak of God or to God. It is definitely through words and thoughts, through the measure of their exactness, that we approach God. This brings us back to the great law of mediation, which governs creation and redemption and which culminates in the incarnation of Christ: our knowledge of God is always mediated. In other words, it is always transmitted and expressed within the realities of this world and through human faith and intelligence. But God infinitely exceeds that knowledge; at the same time he is closer to us than knowledge.

Words and learning can be a snare: "All concepts formed by reason to try to reach and embrace the nature of God succeed only in fashioning an idol; it is not God whom they proclaim," said Gregory of Nyssa.[21] Wonder alone grasps something. We constantly risk objectifying and enclosing God in ideas, making him a simple projection of our desires or confusing him with what the psychologists call the superego.

Thus, silence, mute admiration, and the very simple intuition that God is present to us and that we are present to him must carry our loving regard beyond that which is speakable.

A regard, we say. It is also a question of making ourselves attentive beyond words and pictures to the still small voice, that noise of the silence as it fades away, at the perception of which Elijah hid his face (1 Kings 19:12 ff).

To see, to hear—those are mere figures of speech. The reality takes place in the half-light of faith. And the more the love of God illumines us as a presence, the more we sense the depth of the shadows in our knowledge before that light.

To be Held in the Hands of God

In this attention to God which is contemplation, we are not merely face to face with God because we neither look nor listen in an external way. The life and presence of God envelops us and moves through us. This is already true because we are creatures; it is even more true because of the effect of salvation, which restores the movement of creation from within.

Saying that we are within the life of God signifies precisely and concretely that our prayers and all our lives, in so far as faith is their dynamism, are situated and must be explicitly situated within the life of the Trinity.

According to the beautiful image of Saint Irenaeus, the economy of salvation must lead us back before the face of the Father in a vision that is joy and glory for us. That work is accomplished by the two hands the Father extends to us: the Son and the Spirit.[22] It is the love of the Father for the Son and the Spirit that puts us in those hands, and it is the love of the Son and of the Spirit for the Father that, in the same movement, carries us toward the face of the Father.

The Spirit brings us to Christ in liberating our attention, in arousing our faith. Each time we read or hear the testimony of Scripture, we begin to discover anew who Jesus Christ is. As we like to say today, we discover that he is "the man for others." Yes, and that is true because he is primarily the man for God and God for man. Contemplation is, therefore, a receptive attention that is awakened by the Spirit; in recognizing our true life as that of Christ, it conforms us to his freedom as the Son and draws us with him to the true Father, he who is beyond our imagination, the Father of Jesus Christ.

And *the Son brings us to the Spirit,* in the sense that the entire earthly life of Jesus prepares for Pentecost. And the Spirit, by reviving our freedom, invents in us and with us, our personal ways of following Christ to the Father, in an immense diversity. He is the Spirit of the Son, but also of the Father. It is he who ineffably cries within us: "Abba! Father!" (Rom. 8:15). He also whispers within us "as living water: come to the Father" (Saint Ignatius of Antioch).[23] He also permits us to say "Jesus is Lord" (1 Cor. 12:3).

It would be good for our contemplation often to be a long invocation to the Son and to the Holy Spirit, an attentive and explicit way of letting us be introduced into that communion of love which is the Trinity of God and of which the Father is the source, the beginning without beginning. It would be good for us to have an acute and almost experiential consciousness of that affirmation of the Apostle: through Christ we "have access in one Spirit to the Father" (Eph. 2:18).

We can see that this is not a question of abstract speculation, but of the essential movement of our meeting with God and of our life in him. For God is, in himself, pure communion, pure relationship of reciprocal giving, pure joy of mutual exchange. It is in communion that he welcomes us by the gift of Christ and the anointing of the Holy Spirit. This also is the key to the profound equilibrium of our lives in truth and freedom. Heresies, false liberties, slavery lie in wait for us far more than we realize, and they are all a contempt for or a lack of attention to one aspect or another of the Triune revelation of God.

To be held in the two hands of the Father: there is nothing more to say in affirming that the only way toward God is the humanity of Jesus, upon which contemplation seeks only to look and listen long. It is not above or outside human life, but within it that we discover the heart of the Father and the power of the Spirit. "Yes, the heart of God the Father with respect to us is indeed that expressed for us by him who has come from his heart," as Saint Bernard said.[24]

Contemplation, at the heart of verbalized prayer and of life, will never be anything—in its initial springing forth or at its culmination—except knowledge of Christ, with the power of his resurrection and the sharing of his sufferings (Phil. 3:10). The power of life at the very heart of suffering, the grace of Easter, as Saint Athanasius wrote, "is absolutely not limited to one time, and the splendor of its radiance never undergoes an eclipse. It is always ready to illuminate the spirit of those who have the desire for it."[25] We shall participate always in the grace of Easter, wrote the same author, "if we feel that this celebration constitutes the be all and end all of our life. Always united to Christ and never separating ourselves from him, we shall say to him: 'Lord, to whom shall we go? You have the words of eternal life' (John 6:68)."[26]

A Knowledge of the Heart

Let us look at contemplation from another of its angles and paradoxes. By pure grace and in the Holy Spirit, contemplation is a capacity for admiration, a reflex of surprise—in other words, a way of coming out of oneself. Coming out of oneself: this is characteristic of Christian prayer, which seeks only to enter into the will of God and humbly, with Jesus, to make his will our food (John 4:34). That last expression is very strong; it signifies an "assimilation" so that God's will becomes man's will. Coming out of oneself is simply to love truly.

However, contemplation does not consist of flitting about in the infinity of space, feeling that one has wings, losing consciousness of self. In this coming out of self, God leads man back to his heart, his "heart" in the biblical sense—the center and spiritual root of the person, the place where all man's faculties converge in a profundity of which he can have only a faint intuition.

As Saint Caesarius of Arles preached: "One does not say to you, go to the east to find charity, sail to the west to find devotion. No, it is within you, to your heart that you are commanded to return and from which you must continually drive out anger. As the prophet said: 'Lay it to heart, you rebels' (Isa. 46:8). Yes, I have said that we do not find what the Lord requires of us in faraway places but within our hearts where he sends us. He has, in effect, placed within us that which he expects of us."[27]

This reminder is important. Contemplation is not exaltation, verging on pride; rather it is a digging deep within the self to rediscover human life as it first burst forth, created by God and grafted onto Christ: God in the most inward part of ourselves, his love at the root of our being—it is there that he awaits us.

Our gaze does not have to conquer the light of God. It can't do that. But it is in the light that God projects onto us by his gaze of love that our gaze catches the light of God. Our knowledge of God is, therefore, indirect; but as such it is neither theoretical nor passive. It comes through our knowledge of ourselves, the knowledge of what we are and become in the sight of God, created in his image, directed by his love. "You will not be able to contemplate the light itself," said Saint Gregory of Nyssa. "But if you rediscover the grace of the image placed within you from the beginning, you will possess in yourself the object of your desires."[28]

"Now that you have come to know God," wrote Paul; but he continued, "or rather to be known by God" (Gal. 4:9). The knowledge of God is a knowledge of love, and that love comes from God and is God. To know God is to know ourselves as loved by him, with all the mobilization of our being which that implies. To know God is nothing other than finding this love kindled by him deep within ourselves and opening ourselves in a response of love.

This is important. We do not know God in a cold objectivity, as something external. The knowledge of God, the knowledge of love, is very different from scientific knowledge; it is analogous to our knowledge of a human person whom we love. One cannot say that we "attain" such knowledge; rather we "receive" it. We enter into such knowledge as the other person opens himself or herself to us, simultaneously changing us.

We are not able to know God in himself, but only in that movement of communion by which he comes to us and into us in order that we may enter into him.

We discover God in his love within us through the very sanctification of our human means of knowledge—intelligence, memory, will, imagination, critical sense, lyricism, and so forth—engaged in love and tranfigured by the Holy Spirit. You might say that God is not before our eyes but in the depths of our seeing. We meet him as the object of our love in the same moment that we recognize him as the subject who creates that love.

In the ninth century, John Scotus put these profound words in the mouth of God: "It is not you who understand me, it is I who, by my spirit, understand myself in you. For you are not a light that subsists by itself, but a participation in the Light that does subsist by itself."[29]

Of course it is not a question of denying that God is an object of knowledge analogous to any other, or of falling into subjectivism as if we could extract knowledge of God from our own depth. No, knowledge of God is given to us, and to that extent it is objective; it is even given to us from outside: "the glory of God in the face of Christ," as we know him by the apostolic witness. But we recognize this glory only to the extent that God has begun to shine in our hearts (2 Cor. 4:6). It is revelation and yet inner knowledge from the heart, inseparable from our movement of love toward God, our progressively transfigured subjectivity.

"Blessed are the pure in heart, for they shall see God" (Matt. 5:8).

To Love God with Passion

In everyday language the word "heart" has a meaning that is less pregnant and less inclusive than the meaning it has in the Bible; essentially it designates man's emotional life and feelings, along with the passions that stir them up. But this entire aspect of man's being, this whole dimension, often so tumultuous and demanding, has both its root and its point of convergence in what Scripture calls the heart. Why must emotions remain alien to prayer? And how can a man suddenly separate himself from his emotions, leaving them outside the door at the time of communion with God?

However, in this area everything is not simple. As Julian Green has noted: "One does not have one heart for human beings and another one for God. Therein lies the problem."[30] Perhaps not everyone will see a problem here, but all must surely feel a tension, a contradiction, a certain uneasiness.

If, in fact, God alone can satisfy us, and if the ground of our reason for existence is to be loved by God and to love God, will not all other love seem to us to be too limited, too narrow, and even disappointing? On the other hand, if our emotions vibrate in profound accord with those of another human person, will they ever be capable of expanding enough to love God?

In our emotional life we understand very well the immense difference between loving God and loving a human person. This is all the more true if the latter goes beyond sympathy or friendship to conjugal love with all its carnal components.

It is, therefore, necessary to speak of two very distinct levels of love. One is the spiritual level of faith, where our emotions are troubled by not being able either to see or to hear; they grope in a strange world where they must learn with difficulty the language as well as the silences. The other level is that of the senses, where our emotions are often too absorbed by sight and sound, too inclined to rush uncontrollably into movements of desire or pull back violently in spontaneous antipathy.

This distinction between two levels is appropriate: God and neighbor do not have a common measure. Yet man has but one heart, one set of emotions. This is why he is not able to separate strictly the two levels; God and neighbor are not separate either. And if love for God does not bring the emotions into play, it remains abstract and impersonal: the self is not committed. In the same way, if love for a human person, in friendship or in marriage, does not have a spiritual dimension, if it is not fashioned and guided by at least a human faith, it will simply become a degraded and degrading lust.

Therefore, even theoretically, it is not so easy to distinguish these two levels of love; first, because a man's sensibility is one and, further, because it is placed between two keyboards. It must play on both in very different ways. All human love, to be true and to remain human, must have a divine dimension. And love for God is authentic only if it retains fully human roots and, therefore, a certain analogy with man's way of loving other human persons. And yet what a difference there is between these two loves! Not merely of degree, but of radically different orders.

If, from a rather theoretical reflection on this double commitment of man's emotions, we now move on to the specific way in which they react, we can perhaps understand what Julian Green meant in speaking of a problem. In principle and in truth, God and man do not compete with one another. We know that, but do we really know it in our hearts?

In fact, man's emotions do not voluntarily give way to the analyses and reasons of his intelligence. They interact all together and cannot fragment themselves without exhaustion. Also the emotions, perhaps even more than the other forces that make up a human being, risk bringing everything back to themselves and loving the self through the objects of emotion. If the emotions are kindled for a human person, will not God be forgotten? And if the emotions are kindled toward God, is it really God whom one loves? To make an idol of the beloved human person and to reduce God to our measure: these are the constant and contradictory tendencies of man's emotions.

It is downright dismaying. In order to love God, are we not reduced to offering him those troubled emotions, which are so limited, so ambiguous, so quickly distracted, and so little in accord with his holiness? But it is necessary to recognize that the intellect (insofar as it is distinguishable from the emotions) is no less limited and ambiguous in knowing God. Besides, if the heart is unworthy of God, it must also be unworthy of the neighbor.

Remember the close relation between prayer and action. We do nothing worthwhile or lasting in this life without some enthusiasm, without a certain passion, without engaging our emotions. So also we will not love God if we have no passion or enthusiasm, if we lack a youthfulness and naiveté of the heart recalling that of an engaged couple. "Blessed are those who love God as a man loves his fiancée," said a monk of the early centuries.

This is certainly full of risks—the risk of sentimentality; even more, the risk of the hidden search for self that is included in all emotion. So our passion for God must be sanctified and corrected, since it always tends to turn in on itself. It must be sanctified in its very attachment to God, sanctified by an authentic and widening knowledge of that God who dwells always beyond all knowledge. It must be sanctified and purified not by extinguishing itself but by moving beyond itself.

Nonetheless, the sensibilities and the emotions are among the forces that constitute us. Without them, transfigured by the Holy Spirit yet remaining fully human, we would not love God with all our strength (Mark 12:30); in fact we would hardly love him at all. Assuredly that love, like all love, must move beyond the level of the senses. But is it not first the senses that perceive love, diffusing it in the intelligence and the will? Is it not the senses that concentrate our regard, nurture fervor, freshness of love, and the quest for peace?

* * * * *

Unique by virtue of its object, who is also its author, our passion for God can still not detach itself entirely from that which seethes in our depths. All kinds of thirsts, desires, cravings, disappointments are within us. It is not a question of repressing them. The raw character of life within us is not to be escaped or destroyed; rather it must be accepted with realism.

With respect to our love for God, our passions play first the role of a parable for us: the parable of the thirst for God. Think of all that we are capable of suffering and ready to sacrifice when a passion takes hold of us—all the more so if it is an evil passion.

But all these thirsts have still another function,

going far beyond the function of a parable. As far as possible, and in a continuing renewal, these thirsts must be delved into—from the very reason that gives birth to them up to their utmost pole, so that they manifest themselves clustered as one single thirst: the thirst for being. This is not yet the thirst for God, but it is ready to become so. It is impossible for us to love God without a spark that comes from him, but what that spark ignites within us is nothing other than our powers to love and to desire. These are always in the process of dispersing themselves and mistaking their objects; they must continually be refocused and arranged according to their true perspectives.

"And do not get drunk with wine," Paul wrote to the Ephesians, adding, with a surprising audacity, "but be filled with the Spirit" (Eph. 5:18). As if one replaces the other? Oh, no! He is not comparing the Spirit of God with alcohol, but with what man seeks in alcohol: the feeling of freedom, of grandeur that only the Spirit can give! The argument of the Apostle is not moralistic but spiritual. It does not condemn the desire for drunkeness as such but reminds us not to mistake the source of that thirst, which only the Holy Spirit can assuage. The Fathers of the Church often referred to that passage of Paul, speaking of the "sober drunkenness" that the presence of the Spirit incites within the believer.

Make no mistake about it: this requires a great inner control, a great lucidity and prudence. Fire or water under pressure are not playthings. However, contemplation must descend into the inflammable part of ourselves, into our capacity for passion, in

100

order to be transformed into love. Converting our desires and thirsts is not stunting their growth; on the contrary, it pushes them to a higher plane. "Increase my desire," prayed Saint Anselm, "and give me that which I ask; even if you were to give me all that you have created, it would not suffice for your servant, unless you give yourself."[31] And Divo Barsotti wrote: "One does not choose God because there is nothing else, but it is because one chooses God that there is nothing else."[32]

When we do this, we will also know how to love the world and our neighbors in a true manner, as God loves them, with a holy passion.

* * * * *

To love God with passion, with a passion led beyond itself by faith, yes, but there is more to be said. The emotions do not necessarily allow themselves to be seized and entirely sanctified. Perhaps certain aspects of the emotions were warped during infancy; perhaps some dimensions of the emotional life became atrophied or paralyzed, and now little can be done about it. If, for example, someone appears incapable of believing that anyone could love him, for some reason hidden in his past, that incapacity will have repercussions in his relationship with God. It will not only have repercussions but will amplify itself in the very measure of his desire to love God. The risk is that God will imperceptibly take on the savage face of the unconscious hatred or contempt a man may have for himself.

Yes, there is a problem in having but one heart. But the way of contemplation and love of God is still not blocked. It is only more rugged. For, whatever the state of our emotions, more or less serene or more or less troubled, we can always discover in faith that "God is greater than our hearts" (1 John 3:20) and has a tenderness and generosity inversely proportionate to the feeble idea we can get of him.

*   *   *   *   *

Perhaps having but one heart for both God and neighbor is man's problem; certainly it involves a serious tension. Even without opposing each other, the two dimensions of God and neighbor are too different for our emotions to blend easily. But this tension is also an opportunity! We are not able to resolve it by putting our lives among men and our lives in God side by side. The tension passes through our heart, it traverses our prayer, and it demands an inner unity, which we seek and await as a grace—perhaps the supreme grace.

Escape in God?

Deep within us there is a need for intimacy that God alone can fill. Also there is a more or less conscious desire to be consoled, sheltered, embraced, and loved tenderly. That desire is often expressed in the Psalms: God our shelter, our refuge, our armor, our rock, our fortress, our tabernacle, the wings that cover us. But one immediately sees modern man frown: religion, escape, refusal to face life, infantile repression. Yes, these risks are only too real, and it is good that the political and psychological criticisms of religion make us wary of them.

However, it is not necessary to pretend to be stronger than we really are. Who is able to boast that he is perpetually alert, in a continual state of confrontation, in constant control of his energies —without shriveling up or hardening, without becoming weary or discouraged? If God is not our refuge and strength, something else will be; if we are not held in his arms, it will be somewhere else. In fact, anything can serve as a means of escape —even struggle, revolution and, most especially, protest.

If it is truly *God* in whom we seek refuge, we know very well that the shelter that God offers us within himself has the unique quality of being at the center of our existence as well as at the very end of its trajectory. Finding welcome in the arms of God, on the breast of Jesus, like John at the Last Supper, is first transforming escape into repose, seeing ourselves brought back to what is essential. Then, it is being thrown back into the race. For, as we have seen, finding welcome in God, finding God, is never to find satisfaction; rather it is to be driven by our thirst to finding him more than ever, as our true life.

Furthermore we should not be too quick to call this escape when, in truth, it may be the very opposite—a way of accepting the solitude inherent in being a human person. In all community life and with the most sociable of beings, there is a dimension of the person that remains incommunicable, a back country where the individual is alone, like Jacob at the ford of Jabbok (Gen. 32:22). Even in the most harmonious married life, in the most intimate and compatible love, that impassable distance, that mystery of each being is quite real and more keenly felt because of the love. This verse of Aragon[33] expresses it well:

It is she present in my arms and nevertheless
More absent for being there, and I more lonely,
Being so near to her mystery.

That solitude is painful, and sometimes it makes one afraid, when it is experienced as a limitation that affects all friendship, all human communion. One is tempted then to try to escape from it, to forget it in the bustle of noise and agitation. However, that solitude is the reverse side of what makes each man a unique person. To escape from it is to fail oneself, to seek a lumping together with others rather than a communion. For communion between human persons consists precisely in accepting and respecting that limit, that "elsewhere" of each person.

It so happens that this "elsewhere" is precisely the place of privilege where God awaits us. If our communion with him is limited, the limit comes from us. But the inner solitude of each person is not a limit for God. On the contrary, it is he who gives rise to and calls forth this irreducible originality, together with the margin of human solitude that invariably accompanies it. That human solitude is, finally, the very sign of his call, the depth in which it resounds. To find shelter in God, to make of him our rock, is to give that solitude its positive meaning. Man must not try to escape from it or shut himself up within it; he must recognize and accept the fact that the more he is of God and in God, the more he is truly himself.

Certainly what I have called the inherent solitude in every human person must be carefully distinguished from the impulse of fear or selfishness that ends in hiding from or denying oneself to others. In practice, the distinction is not always easy to make. This solitude of the person is situated beyond the ego, in that depth of self which is known only indirectly. Only faith can reveal this depth, at the moment when a man, rather than lamenting this solitude as a disability, recognizes it as the presence of God and the inner path of communion.

"The day when we understand that the incurable split between ourselves and others is the location of that which makes us—through all the loves, all the influences, all the surroundings—the ourselves that we are, when we understand that it is in this same place that God speaks to us in calling us by name, then we have made the great about-face which turns the solitude of misfortune into the solitude of blessing" (Madeleine Delbrêl).[34]

A Kind of Death

If we confess with the Apostle: "For to me to live is Christ" (Phil. 1:21), and if contemplation is the pivotal time when that certainty takes shape in our lives, another question follows inevitably. Why are we generally more inclined to avoid contemplation despite everything? Why don't we have to make an effort not to remain at it all the time? Why do most of us have more trouble beginning to pray than quitting?

Speaking of Christ, Madeleine Delbrêl says: "We are so made that we are not able to prefer you without a slight combat, so that you, my Beloved, will always be put in balance with that fascination, that exhausting obsession with trifles."[35]

It is not a question here of our human and Christian commitments, of our service to neighbor, of competing claims made on our time. Obsession with trifles is an escape into insignificance, which we seek despite being certain from experience that if we pay the price, especially the price in time, contemplation will not disappoint us. Even if we disappoint ourselves in prayer, God himself will not disappoint us. He is present. He lets himself be found. He opens to him who knocks. He is always going ahead of us to the rendezvous.

Then why do we have this desire to escape into trifles? Why this hesitation, why this sometimes sudden need to find almost any pretext to do something else? Is it only spiritual laziness or a taste for convenience?

As has often been said, we may have a real fear of meeting God because his grace is always also a demand. In truth, it is no small thing for a person who is aware of his sin and who is devoted to himself to say to God, "Thy will be done." Contemplation confronts us with the degree of readiness God expects of us and with the limits we have set up against him. To pray is, therefore, to renounce self, to be converted to God not only for the length of time of the

106

prayer, but also for the slice of existence upon which it shines. Thus we can understand the hesitation that can seize us at the moment of prayer.

But this hesitation may well have another, more hidden cause. To some extent, don't we experience death by entering into communion, into the self-emptying of this sort of prayer? And I mean death as a real thing—an entrance into the unknown, a loss of all that which reassures us in our small personal universes, a return to only that which we are within ourselves, without anything to give illusion or diversion. And what if we encounter only emptiness? What if God does not respond but leaves us totally alone with ourselves in that dumb silence? What if we find only nothingness, if nothing happens to happen?

Yes, it really seems that we always approach contemplation a little like death, as the experience of our limit, of our precariousness, of our dependence, as the experience of the unknown. Contemplation requires that we be able to say with Paul, in a real and precise sense, "to die is gain" (Phil. 1:21). This is the phrase that faith declares, almost against us, that radically puts to the test our love of Christ. Is Christ truly everything to me? And do I truly perceive life apart from him as hardly worth mentioning (Acts 20:24)?

Is this overdramatizing the situation? I think not. The threshold of contemplation is a test of faith, difficult in varying degrees from day to day. Entering into the intimacy of God requires daring to confront an emptiness: an interior emptiness, where the person, its action, and its use of time all become relative. And an emptiness that one wonders if God is going to fill.

Gabriel Widmer has said it well: "The knowledge of God seems like a gift or a conquest to those who do not fear the tension between light and darkness. It is the lot of the strong and persevering, who do not fear the indefinable roughness of the divine reality."[36]

This is the ancient biblical teaching: man cannot see God and live. Neither can man hope and desire to see God without entering into a certain kind of death, which is the condition of man's true life, the way of his resurrection with Christ.

Therefore, it is not surprising that prayer, especially what I have called contemplation, does not just happen all by itself. The power and the desire to know God, the taste for and the courage of communion must be asked for as a grace, a sort of miracle. And to ask for these things, one must want them.

Vigilance and Prayer

Saint Caesarius has said: "Who would be able, without any trouble, to persevere in prayer and find time for reading Scripture? Yes, who would be able to accomplish all that without the grace of God, and without a great application of the heart?"[37]

The exhortations of the New Testament regularly unite prayer with perseverance and vigilance. And that relationship is true in two respects. On one hand, what counts in contemplation is far less its moments of light and its experiences of joy than its fidelity and patient continuity. We have to watch our prayer, to do everything to make it persevering and untiring; we cannot naively depend on spontaneity. In order for prayer to become an authentic freedom, a thrust toward God, what miracles of patience are not necessary?

On the other hand, contemplation is the privileged occasion of vigilance—our way of keeping our eyes open, of keeping our lamps full of oil, of waiting for the master of the house to return at the unknown hour, of discerning the signs of the coming of the Kingdom, of strengthening within us desire for that Kingdom. This means endlessly transforming into ardent hope the disappointment that so often seizes us at still seeing so little of the face of God; it is a process of transforming the pain and burden we sometimes experience in prayer into a passionate waiting.

Do we fear that contemplation will become monotonous? It is a risk to run—rather, a test to undergo. Perhaps we will not know each time how to live contemplation in its unfailing newness and adventure. Necessarily it takes on some of the color of our days, with many contrasts or much uniformity, according to individual temperament, or the point in time, or an individual's spiritual dynamism and attention to the newness of the Spirit. In the midst of a series of gray days we can remind ourselves that we do not start over again as if it were a race: our days and efforts are cumulative.

NOTES

1. A.M. Bernard, *Propos intempestifs sur la prière* (Paris 1969), pp. 50–51.

2. Francis de Sales, "Sermon pour le quatrième dimanche du carême," in *L'Oraison,* Cahiers de la Vie Spirituelle (Paris 1947), p. 91.

3. Anonymous, Letter, September 1969.

4. Augustine, *On the Trinity,* XV, 2.

5. D. Molinié, *Le Combat de Jacob* (Paris 1967), p. 28.

6. Dorotheus of Gaza, *Oeuvres spirituelles,* Instruction IV, 48.

7. Bernard, *For the Epiphany,* Sermon I.

8. Paul Claudel, *La messe là-bas* (Paris 1939), p. 55.

9. Bernard, *On the Canticle,* Sermon 84, 1.

10. *Ibid., On Consideration,* V, XI, 24.

11. Caesarius, Sermon 151, 1 (Edition Corpus Christianorum).

12. Philaretus, cited in V. Lossky, *Essai sur la théologie mystique de l'Eglise d'Orient* (Paris 1944), p. 48.

13. Georges Lefebvre, *The Wellsprings of Prayer,* trans. Kathleen Pond (Tournai: Desclée, 1960), p. 41.

14. *Ibid.,* p. 44.

15. Ignatius of Antioch, *On the Epistle to the Ephesians,* XV, 2.

16. See A. Vergotte, "Le nom de Dieu à l'écart de la topologie symbolique," in *L'Analyse du langage théologique: le nom de Dieu* (Paris 1969), pp. 266 f.

17. Karl Barth, *Evangelical Theology: An Introduction,* trans. Grover Foley (New York: Holt, Rinehart and Winston, 1963), p. 164.

18. Dionysius the Areopagite (Pseudo-Dionysius), *Treatise on the Divine Names,* VII, 3.

19. *Ibid.,* Letter V to Dorotheus.

20. D. Molinié, *op. cit.,* p. 135.

21. Gregory of Nyssa, *The Life of Moses,* Theory II, 165.

22. Irenaeus, *Against the Heresies, IV, 20, 1.*

23. Ignatius of Antioch, *On the Epistle to the Romans,* VII, 3.

24. Bernard, *For the Epiphany,* Sermon II, 4.

25. Athanasius, *Epistle V,* 1.

26. *Ibid., Epistle VII,* 1.

27. Caesarius of Arles, Sermon 37, 1.

28. Gregory of Nyssa, "Sixième homélie sur les Béatitudes," *Les Chemins de Dieu* (Paris 1957), pp. 127–128.

29. John Scotus, *Homily on the Prologue of St. John,* ch. 13.

30. Julian Green, *Le bel aujourd'hui* (Paris 1958), p. 317.

31. Anselm, *Meditation,* XIV, 2.

32. Divo Barsotti, *Dieu est Dieu* (Paris 1967), p. 195.

33. Louis Aragon, "Cantique à Elsa," *Les yeux d'Elsa* (Neuchâtel 1945), p. 95.

34. Madeleine Debrêl, "Le silence de la ville," *Christus* (French) 49, p. 8.

35. *Ibid., La Joie de croire* (Paris 1968), p. 94.

36. Gabriel Widmer, "Clarté et ambiguité de la connaissance de Dieu," *Foi et Vie* (1967), Numbers 2–3.

37. Caesarius of Arles, Sermon 236, 4.

4

Prayers of petition

The prayer of petition raises special problems today. One can agree that prayer can be viewed as a presence of God, an attention to his love, and yet remain perplexed as to what is proper to say or not to say in prayer. One can also freely accept the idea of praising God, or easily recognize the necessity of confessing our misery to him, without knowing clearly what one should ask of him for oneself or for others.

In fact, for us prayer of petition is very dependent on the way we view the relationship between God and the world. Of all the forms of prayer, petition is the one most attacked by modern criticism; it is also the one most misrepresented. I shall, therefore, expand certain reflections from the first chapter in order to examine the conditions of authentic petition.

First, however, there is another road to walk, in order to avoid, if possible, accommodating petition to the tastes of the day, or even unconsciously keeping a certain distance from it. To a great extent is not the vigor and the depth of our faith to be measured precisely by our manner of asking for favors?

Does God Answer Our Prayers?

One thing is certain. When the New Testament exhorts us to pray with perseverance, confidence, and assurance, it is speaking primarily of petitions. The great promise it announces in this connection is that God answers those who rely on him. The parables of the importunate friend who insists until his neighbor gives him bread in the middle of the night (Luke 11:5 ff), and of the widow who wore out the judge until he granted her plea (Luke 18:1 ff) conclude, as do others: even more will your Father in heaven hear and grant your prayers (Luke 11:13; 12:27–30; Matt. 7:11).

Now it is precisely about this granting of prayers that Christians today—even some of those who have no particular crisis of faith—have enormous difficulty being sure. Many Christians, in their prayers or in the way they speak, seem almost anxious in advance to excuse God from hearing them. They avoid precise prayer as if to leave a way out in case the prayer is not granted.

Are we to assume this to be a lack of faith? Yes, but not too quickly, for faith has nothing to do with the Coué method.* We are frequently pulled about, if not torn apart, between the wish to have confidence in God and the awareness that we have not received what we asked. We are then tempted to subtract from prayer all requests that touch on ma-

* Coué is well known for saying "Everything in every way is getting better and better." [Trans.]

114

terial realities. But isn't that an escape into a kind of skepticism or a way of limiting the lordship of God over all things?

In reality, if one is forced to conclude that he has not been heard, is this abandoning faith? Faith should not be blind, for it must not affirm something that doesn't exist. But neither is faith a confidence to be measured by human limits. It truly becomes itself when, facing what seems to be evidence of not being heard, it refuses to give up. Renouncing what seems obvious, it pushes its confidence and hope on beyond. Not accepting defeat, it enters lucidly into at least a momentary obscurity. Hoping against all hope, it continues to the end preferring to argue with God and even—while trembling—to test him, rather than accepting the notion that God is not able to reply.

In truth it is risky and even suspect to discourse about the answering of prayer and its conditions. This is a mystery that one confronts sharply in prayer, not a problem that lends itself to argument. This is the testing of our confidence in the promises of the gospel, not an object of rational analysis.

Certainly, prayer must be purified, must guard itself against the numerous counterfeits that lie in wait for it. And in that, reason has its role to play. But reason will not resolve the question of the answering of our prayers. So let us not transform into a problem to be resolved that which is a mystery derived from the life of faith, of intimacy between God and man.

The New Testament is explicit. It is good to bear that in mind and not to deviate from its promises:

115

"Ask, and it will be given you . . . . If you then, who are evil, know how to give good gifts to your children, how much more will your Father who is in heaven give good things to those who ask him!" (Matt. 7:7, 11).

"Whatever you ask in prayer, believe that you have received it, and you will" (Mark 11:24).

And in John: "Hitherto you have asked nothing in my name; ask and you will receive" (John 16:24). " . . . that you should go and bear fruit and that your fruit should abide, so that whatever you ask the Father in my name he may give it to you" (John 15:16). "If you ask anything in my name, I will do it" (John 14:12).

One Does not Skimp on Faith

We must begin by facing up to a fundamental principle. First of all, prayers of petition grow out of faith—faith as something beyond sensory experience, and faith as a challenge to limited and superficial views of reality. Prayer is audacious, not weakness, if it does not falter before the lack of human evidence for God's answer, nor before the apparent insignificance of the cry that it raises in the night. In short, if it does not skimp on faith.

This is clear in the following text. (The first paragraph is all the more striking since the quotation is from Saint Bernard,[1] whose spiritual life was especially luminous and shot through with transcendence.)

> Whenever I begin to speak of prayer, it seems to me
> that I can hear the thoughts of your hearts asking the

116

question which has often been put to me by others, and which I have sometimes felt stirring in my own mind: "How is it that although we pray almost without ceasing, we hardly ever appear to derive any fruit from our prayers?" We seem to be just the same after our prayers as we were before. No one has replied a word to us, no one has given us anything for our trouble; and it appears that we have been laboring in vain.

But what says the Lord in the Gospel?

"Do not judge by appearance, but judge with right judgment" (John 7:24). And what is right judgment if not one of faith? For it is written, "He who through faith is righteous shall live" (Gal. 3:11). Put your trust therefore in the judgment of faith and not in your own experience, because faith is infallible where human experience is likely to err. But where shall we find the truth of faith if not in the promises given to us by the Son of God himself: "Whatever you ask in prayer, believe that you have received it, and you will" (Mark 11:24).

My brethren, none of you ought to look upon his own prayers as of little value, for I assure you that he to whom they are addressed does not regard them so. Before the prayer has time to leave your lips he orders it to be registered in his own book. And when we pray we can always hope with confidence for one or the other of two things. Either he will give us what we ask, or we shall receive something else which he knows will be more profitable for us. For "we do not know how to pray as we ought" (Rom. 8:26), but God has compassion on our ignorance, and while he graciously receives our prayers, he refuses to give us what would not be good for us, or defers to grant what should preferably be given later on. Our prayer, however, does not remain unfruitful.

No, one does not skimp on faith, faith understood as a confidence in God obstinately taking God at his word. And in that confidence we cannot let ourselves think that there are parts of life too commonplace for God's concern or too material for him to reveal his power and glory in them.

Aren't we able to ask anything at all of God? Yet, we know in advance that there are inappropriate prayers, prayers that God is unable to answer, not because they are too precise and concrete, but because they revolve too much around ourselves and because they would make of God a distributor of goods for our use. This is what James says: "You ask and do not receive, because you ask wrongly, to spend it on your passions" (James 4:3).

So we cannot simply say that faith must be a limitless confidence in God. It is also necessary to make clear that faith must be a way of entering into the purposes of God, instead of trying to get God to enter into ours. "In my name," said Jesus, when he exhorted the disciples to ask and promised that they would be answered (John 15:16; 14:12). To pray in his name is to adhere to the very meaning of his life on earth: the coming of the Kingdom of God. To pray in his name is to order our needs and desires to the will of God: gathering us into his Kingdom. This is the originality of Christian prayer, "a call from God to God, having for foundation his revealed plan."[2]

So we are able to ask anything for ourselves, on any level, providing it is with a view to keeping watch for the coming of the Kingdom, to working for its coming, to being witnesses to Christ or, as Jesus said, bearers of a living fruit. We are also able to ask for anything for other persons, for a neighbor or for all mankind, if our hope for them is ultimately the Kingdom, that which God desires for them.

In prayer, the childish infinity of our needs must give way to an openness to the infinity of love of which Christ is the witness and we are the fellow laborers. Prayer is then asking "God to enter into his care for the world."[3]

From the depths of prison, Bonhoeffer wrote:

> God does not grant all our desires, but he fulfills all of his promises. This is to say that he remains the Lord of the world, that he sustains his Church and gives us faith ever anew; that he does not give us a burden too heavy to carry, but fills us with his presence and with his help; that he answers our prayers and brings us to himself by the best and straightest path. In doing that faithfully, he has a right to our praises.
>
> All that we have any right to expect from God and to ask in our prayers is found in Jesus Christ . . . . It is necessary for us to try to enter ever more intimately and very calmly into the life, the words, the acts, the sufferings, and the death of Jesus in order to recognize what God promises and what he accomplishes.[4]

FOUR QUESTIONS

So the prayer of petition must be measured not by its problems, but by its *mystery,* a mystery that was not any easier to live in other historical ages of the Church. Now let's consider the questions that are most asked in our times about such prayer. A group of couples who have been trying to discuss the most important of our current perplexities have formulated four such questions:

Is it necessary to ask God for what we expect from science and technology?

Is it honest to pray without being able to act?

Why ask if God knows everything?

Is petition a persevering struggle or a confident surrender to the will of God?

> *Is it necessary to ask God*
> *for what we expect from*
> *science and technology?*

Behind this question lies both a repugnance for magical prayer and a refusal to return, in prayer, to a naive and infantile attitude unrelated to modern scientific knowledge and today's conception of the world. Inevitably all this poses the question of the relationship between the active presence of God in his creation and the framework of laws that science is uncovering and upon which technology is based.

God Is not One Cause among Many

The material world appears to us as a web of causes and effects over which man presently is acquiring greater and greater power. As men of the twentieth century, we cannot believe that God would intervene among these causes as one among many. But as Christians, knowing what we do about God, we cannot believe that he is situated among the laws that rule the world, we cannot imagine him as a mechanic pulling the levers of his machine or as an operator of an electronic computer punching the keys.

Man's technological possibilities, despite their sensational progress, are still limited and, perhaps, will remain so. Will the intervention of God, therefore, be at the fringes of human limits, where man can do nothing? Does prayer begin where our powerlessness begins? That would make God into a stopgap—and one whose domain will likely go on shrinking. That idea is unbearable for both the Christian faith and the critical intelligence. It would be unworthy of both God and man as they are revealed in Christ.

The universe, which now appears to us to be very strong in its self-consistency, in a certain autonomy, and in its chain of determinisms, has been created this way by the will of God. Science has not obtained its status in opposition to God, but in opposition to the confusion that Christians have often made between their faith and an outdated conception of the world.

The World Is not Closed in on Itself

If science obliges us to think of the world as purely deterministic, absolutely closed in on itself, then prayer will be seen as excluded from the material world. It would be the same if we had to think that reality is strictly limited to what is apprehended by science. It would also be the same if we had to conclude that technology, once deployed to its greatest potential, has sufficient and exclusive competence to solve all our earthly problems.

Such conclusions are not, in fact, by any means required by science, and those persons who adopt such views of technology do so in the name of materialist or positivist faiths. The self-consistency of material reality is not to be denied; but, far from reducing it to a blind and oppressive determinism, we can very well think of it as open to God and, thus, in relationship with him. Prayer, then, will embody the belief that a divine plan mysteriously envelopes the totality of the world's material laws, a divine plan that has willed those laws and gives them meaning.

As for the power of technology—operating on its own terrain—we should not try to impose limits on it. Far from replacing human responsibility, technology in fact requires it and greatly increases it. Technology constitutes the grip of man upon the material world; but man goes beyond that material world. Within the Christian perspective he is, as it were, at the hinges of the relationship between God and the world.

However perfected it may be, technology remains but the tool whose use depends on men and women, for better or worse. And for a Christian, that use must be in the service of human beings and of the human race and is directly bound to the meaning that God gives to life and to human history. The role of prayer does not consist in replacing technology nor in rivaling it, but in seeing that it is used as the servant of man—more precisely, as the servant of God's plan to unite mankind in his love.

That said, prayer attests indirectly to the fact that technology does not have its end in itself; it is not an absolute. Prayer also attests to the fact that man does not have the ultimate responsibility for the world because he remains incapable of giving meaning to it. Man's responsibility, great and admirable as it is, is like that of a steward or manager —although one who enjoys the confidence of the owner and is even invited to live in intimacy with him.

Coincidence and Miracle

If we are tempted today to limit petitions to what concerns man's inner life and the spiritual realities, it is because we can have some idea of the way in which God is present to persons. It is infinitely more difficult for us to imagine how God is present in the impersonal world, most notably within those coincidences which seem to be fortunate or unfortunate for us.

The naive inclination is to think that everything that happens is directly organized and positively determined by God. But is God to be seen as an immense station-master of all circumstances, creating or suppressing events willy-nilly? Does he hold back or advance processes arbitrarily? Such a vision contradicts science and, more simply, experience. Further, it leads to that absurd and scandalous attitude which tries to see the punitive or beneficent hand of God behind everything that happens. Recall how Jesus answered those who asked about the accident at the tower of Siloam and the executions ordered by Pilate (Luke 13:1–5).

One can say that all events challenge us on behalf of God. But it is our way of reacting to each event, of giving it a meaning that makes it a blessing or a threat. That does not mean that all events are a direct intervention of God in our existence.

The rationalist argument, on the other hand, is simply the reverse of this naive tendency: whatever happens results from an infinite chain of cause and effect with no relation to God. But from a Christian perspective does this not render insignificant both the material world and our life in that world?

In both cases the error consists of forging a simple and generalized theory—everything comes directly from God or nothing comes from him—a theory that is far broader than what we are able to know. It is very important that our reason and prayer take into account this ignorance and preserve this mystery. Without our knowing how, God is present in this world that science explores and technology seeks to master, present in the world's history and evolution. It is, of course, an intimate presence, but unimaginable, of another order and, perhaps, very different from case to case. It can happen, however, that we see a specific coincidence, a particular chain of events, as being directly consonant with God's design for ourselves personally or for a whole group of persons. That would be the miracle: a surprising occurrence, which may, perhaps, be more or less explainable by reason but which cannot help suddenly becoming a sign for faith.

The Providence of God

Prayer presupposes, therefore, faith in the providence of God. It also presupposes that we have a certain understanding of that providence and that we are able to discern the will of God, certainly not in everything, but at least in certain events.

But suppose I try to discern the will of God in some event, in order to *then* find in that event a meaning for my own life. That effort will certainly result in an illusion. On one hand, the general relationship between the will of God and events escapes us; on the other hand, a fact does not become an event for me except to the extent that it affects me and I make it my own. In other words, an event has a subjective dimension.

In consequence, it seems that no event (suffering, accusation, success) can be understood as expressing the will of God for me except *through the way in which I receive it,* through trying to give it meaning that is first of all human.

In other words, the questions we ask ourselves about providence cannot be given objective answers. The providence of God includes and elevates to primacy the freedom of human beings and their reaction as responsible persons. This is why I cannot discern the effects of providence as a spectator from outside, but only through the way in which a specific event concerns me personally.

Not that God's will is reduced to mine, nor that his providence is reduced to the meaning I give to the event. But still God and his plan for me are not of the order of an object that is accessible to a neutral regard or understanding. Providence is a movement of God toward man, an aspect of his love; man is not able to know that movement, unless he lets himself be met and taken along by it.

We would very much like it if providence turned out to be a mechanism, on the level of things. But we discover it is a communion, a personal presence of God with man. This discovery must become our point of view on things, and also the motive and mood of our prayer.

Our prayer of petition will not put in doubt the fact that everything proceeds from God in one way or another; indeed, that is precisely the mystery that it must preserve. If we met the providence of God only in events that happen, perhaps we would not dare to ask for anything at all, fearing to make a mistake. But we know that God is also—even first of all—with us in facing these events, in order to give them a meaning. So we can express our petition with confidence and realism, without fearing that it will prejudice the meaning of an event or will treat God as a building superintendent or stage manager.

"I believe," wrote Bonhoeffer, "that God is not an agent of fate standing outside of time, but that he hears our sincere prayers and sees our responsible actions and responds to them."[5]

Prayer without Naiveté or Skepticism

Without making a general theory, I can say that prayer is showing a twofold respect: a rational respect for the consistency characteristic of the world, and a spiritual respect for the secret presence of God in this world. Thus, prayer is desiring and asking that the will of God, which is his love, be realized in and through the texture of laws and the

126

chain of causes. So, for example, I can pray, without naiveté or skepticism, for a cure or for the resolution of some conflict, things that depend on laws that are the object of scientific (psychosociological) knowledge and of technological action.

Can I pray for some material reality that technology cannot yet accomplish—say, rain or good weather? Answering "no" to that question would be naively insisting that God's power is measured by the limits of human technology. To the extent that the rain and sun are vital necessities to man and, therefore, are an authentic concern, should not that concern be expressed in prayer? It will, moreover, be a prayer that includes man's hope that mastery of atmospheric phenomena will be forthcoming. Additionally, it will be a prayer that leaves entirely aside the question of knowing how meteorological laws can serve God's love for his people.

For one does not pray for things, one prays for persons. But one never stops believing that the material life of those persons (and their relationship to things and events) is not alien to the communion of love that God has created between them and him. And one asks that everything work for the good of those for whom one prays (Rom. 8:28), without, however, knowing if that good will be realized objectively or subjectively, directly or indirectly in their experience of events.

Prayer risks being an attempt at magic if we try to make God intervene in place of technology or within the gaps in our scientific knowledge. One might say symbolically that prayer must not aim at

127

making God descend into things or among things, but at presenting God with the entire context of our life on earth, relating it all to him in an act of confidence and hope. That sort of prayer situates the individual within the dynamism of the spiritual unification of all creation in Christ (Eph. 1:10).

Summary

God and technology: we see here neither competition nor two realms that are alien to, opposed to, or exclusive of one another. They are two radically different but not separate orders: the order of this world and its technology and the order of the plan of God, which invisibly envelopes the former while remaining itself.

It is right and necessary to ask God in different but complementary ways for those things which we expect from man's technology; it is equally right and necessary to seek to accomplish, as far as possible, through technology those things we ask of God. It is all the same world—for us it is as much the domain of science as the gift of grace. It is the same man who trusts in God and who exercises worldly responsibility (which he has received from God). It is the same concern that calls forth both prayer and the employment of technology: the concern for peace, for justice, for health, for a good harvest and a safe voyage, as well as for daily bread.

As an affirmation in act, but also as an ardent desire, the prayer of petition declares that the Kingdom is always infinitely beyond human action and its technology, yet simultaneously the Kingdom

128

is present within that action as its only true and ultimate meaning.

Is it honest to pray
without being able to act?

Prayer–An Alibi?

"Not to work and then to pray to make up for it," wrote Péguy, "I consider to be bad manners."

This quotation suggests the risk that prayer may simply be a way of getting out of our responsibilities easily. In matters not touching directly on our most real, most personal existence, we are so quickly forgetful, so rapidly consoled, and so soon interested in something else. In that respect, prayer easily becomes a way of handing over to God the needs and misfortunes of other people so we won't have to worry about them ourselves. Our limited compassion will have found expression, if not effect, and we will be free from the burden of responsibility. But too many outside critics have hit us at this point to allow us to remain oblivious of the pitfall.

If intercession consists of our asking to enter into the will of God for mankind, it commits us seriously. Its fervor can only be measured by the extent of our real availability for action. As Monsignor Anthony Bloom has said, intercession does not consist in "politely calling to God's attention what he has forgotten to do."[6] It consists in taking a step toward the heart of tragic situations: it unites us with Christ incarnate, with God turned toward humanity. Mak-

129

ing the will of God our own in prayer includes holding ourselves ready to become fellow workers with God in action, as Duquoc explains.[7]

To be honest in prayer is a tremendous requirement that must abide in us as a constant challenge, as a way of holding our hearts on the alert, and as a will to do everything possible to live in symbiosis in our prayer and our attention to others.

Prayer Limited to Personal Commitments?

We can never take the need for responsibility proportionate to intercession too seriously. But must I refuse to intercede when I am personally incapable of doing something specific and immediate? Must I limit my prayer to that which is within reach of an efficacious action on my part? Although I am aware of the risks of alibi-prayer, I reply "no" to this question for several reasons.

In our wish to be honest with God and available to our neighbors, the possibilities for personal action remain very limited. Very often there is really no possibility at all. In such cases prayer can remain authentic because it places confidence in the power of God, which is of another order than ours and doesn't have our limitations. But this is true only so long as prayer keeps itself open to any possibilities for action that might be discovered later on.

Additionally, is one ever reduced to saying absolutely, "There is nothing I can do"? If we dare to entrust to the love of God those problems which are vastly beyond our capacities to solve, such as peace or justice, we can do so honestly only in the knowledge that at least on our own level we must be workers for peace and justice. Our prayer must bring us back to the specific, in order to take a large view without being abstract; back to our immediate and concrete responsibilities, to the texture of our human intercourse, as well as to that larger and more indirect relationship which is political and economic. Everything is interrelated—in a tenuous and usually hidden way—the great causes of humanity and the responsibility that the citizen of a country exercises through the votes he casts and the positions he takes. Intercessory prayer cannot get along without information on the life of the world and a thoughtful and, as far as possible, responsible political attitude.

To Count on Human Unity

In the end, we can honestly pray for causes or for individuals whom we cannot help personally in any way. It is impossible for one individual to be involved on all levels and at all points of the compass at the same time. This is another limit to our presence with others. But other persons become committed where I am not, and they do what I cannot do. They even act for me to the extent that I feel committed for them as I carry out the responsibilities that I have judged to be right and necessary for me to undertake personally.

So, relying on the limited but serious involvement that is properly mine, my prayer can legitimately reach out to emergencies and needs in areas where other men and women are striving to bring answers. In unity with God's plan, intercession makes me more acutely, more newly conscious of the unity of all people on earth, and of that other unity which is the communion of saints in Christ—unity in misfortune and need, but also unity in service and commitment.

Why ask if God
knows everything?

The question seems banal and predictable; however, it is profound and, in reality, is asked most insistently today.

As early as the fourth century, Evagrius said: "I ask of you that no one give advice to our Lord, or say this is what should happen and not that."[8]

As soon as one realizes that intercession does not constitute a means of pressure or, even less, of blackmail, an attempt to twist to his own ends the destiny that God may have fixed for him, he sees the question: what is the reason for prayer? Two questions can be discussed here. From man's point of view, isn't intercession artificial? And from God's view, has such prayer any use or meaning.?

A Relationship of Grace

No, intercession is not artificial on our part, even if it does not pretend to teach God something or to give him advice. It expresses, in a very authentic way, what it first obliges us to recognize: that in our relationship with God we have no rights, nothing is due us; it is a relationship of grace. Miracle does not exist only in the extraordinary; it also exists—and is more widely present—in all the good that happens to us in the usual course of things. The facts that we exist and that God loves us cannot be taken for granted. Prayers of petition express, with simplicity, this attitude which alone can respond to the generosity of God, an attitude of admiring astonishment, of humble recognition, and of love.

God Counts on Our Prayers

God knows better than we do, and before we do, that which we need to ask of him (Matt. 6:8). Does that fact reduce prayer to merely acting as a pedagogue of grace? Or does intercession have a reality or power before God?

Unless we give in to a reductive rationalism, we cannot fail to say with the New Testament that God truly counts on our prayers. This is an aspect of the mystery that confounds us: God's design seriously includes our participation; his plan of creation and salvation takes the form of an authentic cooperation. This cooperation, furthermore, is indescribable and unimaginable, for it does not happen on only one level where God takes one part and we the other. Rather, it operates on two radically different planes, one encompassing the other: that of God in his transcendence, and that of man in his world. God is all, has created all, but in such a way that our participation is intensely real and necessary.

We can well ask ourselves what good our prayer can do—not to mention our faith and our actions—within the secret, hidden way in which God makes all things work together for the good of those who love him, and for the final transfiguration of the creation. But we may not give up believing and saying that truly our prayer, by the power of the Spirit of God in us, is itself like a power that plays its role in the plan of God.

"We do not need to hesitate," wrote Karl Barth,

133

"to say that 'on the basis of freedom of God himself God is conditioned by the prayer of faith.' The basis is his freedom. It is thus a form of his sovereignty."[9] And J. F. Six has said in the same vein: "When you pray, you do not pray to change what God has decided, but to obtain that which he wishes to accomplish by your prayers."[10]

Is God Deterministic?

Our language constantly needs to be corrected. In saying that God knows all, we mean that our prayers do not pretend to instruct God. But that does not necessarily imply that everything, in all detail, is ordered by God in advance in a precise and determined chain.

We do not know how it is. But our experience of life could make us imagine that, in a certain way, God improvises within his process and invents new developments with us, according to the readiness or resistance that we show. This could be the meaning of those biblical statements that God, at a given moment, repented an action, went back on a decision, changed his opinion. Without being captive to these anthropomorphisms, we can sense the truth they suggest; then we can better understand the positive role our intercession plays in the project of God.

For some time now, many Christians have preferred to speak of God's "project" rather than of his "plan of salvation." They have done so specifically to avoid imposing the idea of a divine determinism, projecting onto God the inflexibility of

134

the processes that science discovers in material phenomena. If God's action does not contradict the natural chain of events that he has instituted, that fact does not imply that God himself must submit to such a chain of determined events. History itself —the history of humanity—furnishes us with a better analogy to describe the action of God. It provides the image of a process wherein operate the freedoms of individuals; at the same time there function, each on its own level, the determinations of the laws of the material world, and those of psychology and of sociology.

Is intercession a persevering struggle or a confident surrender to the will of God?

Perhaps the first reaction to this question is to say there is no choice. However, the question expresses a tension that certainly exists within the spiritual life and prayer of each person—a tension that can also be noted in different kinds of spiritual life.

Think of the parables we have already recalled —those of the friend who came in the night to ask his neighbor for bread, and of the insistent widow—as well as of the various cures performed by Jesus because of the persistence with which individuals asked for them. Think, too, of the biblical exhortations for us to persevere in prayer, to struggle in intercession. All that calls up the image of an insistent prayer which asks with audacity, which awaits a precise answer, and which presents itself as a struggle—not necessarily a struggle against God but, perhaps, with God against adversities.

On the other hand, if we refuse to conceive of prayer as an attempt to wrest from God that which he would hesitate to give, if we try to understand prayer as a way for us to make God's will our own, that intention will lead us to experience and to describe intercession as an act of confidence, a movement by which we put ourselves in God's hands.

Two Possible Dangers

It is in their possible deviations that these two spiritual emphases best appear in tension but as necessary complements. The image of struggle, the emphasis on earnest perseverance, certainly expresses faith, in that it makes the believer an intimate of God. But it is a short step from prayer as wrestling with God to prayer as a means of pressure or an act of magic. We find it so easy to make God into a satellite of a center that is ourselves.

But there is an opposite risk, more common in our time. Confident surrender can hide a certain skepticism, can express a vague faith in God, who is distant or somewhere else. Do we dare to trust the promises of God, to count ardently on the seriousness of his commitment to us, to appeal from God to God in the name of his love, as Abraham did before Sodom and Gomorrah (Gen. 18:22)? Or do we experience prayer so well distilled that it is almost nonexistent? Almost as if we hardly dare to stand by what we ask.

136

A Double Movement

Our intercession must always oscillate somewhat between these two emphases. Faith is simultaneously long perseverance and unwavering confidence. If prayer is too much involved with insisting, it no longer addresses itself to the true God; if it is too quickly and too easily confident, it no longer expresses us truly.

Thus, there are two movements, inversely complementary. The order of priority differs according to persons and circumstances.

From Us to God

In one of these movements, prayer goes from man to God, so to speak. It is aroused concretely by a specific need. It surges up from a particular concern, for oneself personally or for others. It expresses an anxiety, a sorrow, a hope, a disappointment, an indignation. Little by little, then, it must center on God, rejoining God's expectation of man. This will be its perseverance. From the cry of a man it must become the word of someone to whom God has made himself known. In this way it will be prayer "in the name of Jesus the Christ, our Savior," the desire to enter into the will of the Father. And through this process, we will become aware that in and beyond all the needs we express, all the human requests that we formulate, it is in fact *God himself* whom we desire and await. Then, as waiting for God, prayer will have become the movement by which man restores himself to him, wishing to live by him and for him.

A modern author, J. F. Six, expresses well this movement of prayer: "For a long time you have asked God to restore the health which you have lost. Through the process of asking you have become transformed into a being-who-asks-of-God. And I have seen with astonishment that you no longer ask him for that health which you missed so badly."[11]

From God to Us

The other movement is that of the Lord's Prayer: the prayer that goes from God to us. From the outset it moves straight to the essential, to the center of reality: may God, as he has made himself known to us by his name, be recognized and adored in his holiness; may his kingdom, already come in Christ, be fully established (that is, may this world soon pass away in those aspects where it is imperfect but, also, in this world may the leaven of the Kingdom rise more and more); may the will of God, which is his love, be done or, in other words, may this communion of life wherein God will be all in all grow and soon be achieved.

Such prayer is totally occupied with God, but it is prayer that commits us intensely, as temples where the name of God is celebrated, as fellow-workers of his Kingdom, as stewards of his will on earth. Also, this prayer necessarily prolongs itself with an intercession for ourselves, petition that places us and our needs within the perspective of service of God and of friendship with Christ. Beyond the reconciliation of pardon and the victorious help of God in our trials and temptations, this prayer leads us to ask for our daily bread. Bread, which means the essence of that which we need to live "here below." The request for bread certainly includes all our material needs, but it excludes the superfluous, the useless cravings, and the desire to build up reserves.

* * * * *

Such are the two complementary movements of a prayer which, without ceasing to be the prayer of an earthly man, does not wish to revolve around man but to rejoin the will of God and his project of salvation. However, these things often do not happen peacefully. The conversion of prayer is slow, difficult, and always to be begun again. It took Jesus hours of anguish and struggle in order to pass from a prayer asking that the cup of death be taken from him, to one that acquiesced in the will of the Father (Mark 13:35 ff). As J.F. Six says: "And we think we can coordinate easily, without sweat or blood, our searching, our will, with those of God."[12]

NOTES

1. Bernard, *On Lent,* Sermon V, 5.
2. Christian Duquoc, "L'Originalité de la prière chrétienne," *Catéchèse* 32 (1968) 270.
3. *Ibid.,* p. 275.
4. Dietrich Bonhoeffer, *Résistance et soumission* (Geneva 1967), p. 184.
5. *Ibid.,* p. 11.

6. Anthony Bloom, "Prier aujourd'hui," *Contacts* No. 61 (1968) 4.

7. Christian Duquoc, *art. cit.*, p. 277.

8. Evagrius, Letter 42, cited in P. Hausherr, *Les leçons d'un contemplatif, le Traité de l'oraison d'Evagre* (Paris 1960), p. 29.

9. Karl Barth, *Church Dogmatics,* trans. T.H.L. Parker, W.B. Johnston, et al; ed. G.W. Bromley and T.F. Torrance (Edinburgh: Clark and New York: Scribners, 1959), Vol. II, Part 1, pp. 510–511.

10. Jean François Six, *La prière et l'espérance* (Paris: Du Seuil, 1968), p. 25.

11. *Ibid.,* p. 91.

12. *Ibid.,* p. 35.

5

Liturgy from day to day

The preceding pages discussed prayer before it becomes diversified in different forms of expression, prayer as the essential attitude of man before God. Therefore, nothing specific was said about common prayer and the liturgy. In this chapter I will do that briefly, looking at the liturgy from a limited angle: that of certain questions and tensions that have arisen in modern renewal movements.

To do so I will refer mostly to the experience of renewal within monastic and religious communities, because the experience of such communities in the liturgy is especially typical of that of other Christian assemblies.

The Relativity of the Liturgy and Its Renewal

The current renewal in liturgical practice is certainly a necessity and a blessing. It is motivated by the desire for authenticity and, therefore, has a double movement: a return to the sources and a wish for modernization. It mobilizes simultaneously a critical spirit and an inventive, creative spirit, with all the attention, even passion, which they necessarily imply. A requirement of truth and simplicity runs through all, calling for research, experiments, mobilization of physical, intellectual, and spiritual forces, and much patience aroused by the will to succeed.

But for all of these reasons, liturgical renewal also involves a trial and a certain number of temptations. It risks seeing novelty as a value in itself and being shot through with a spirit that is not only critical but unilaterally limited and purist. It risks confusing modernization with fads, yielding to ideas that are more overwhelming than well-balanced, exaggerating the break that characterizes our age to the detriment of historical continuities. It also faces the danger of mobilizing too much energy and too much attention and of creating tension, fatigue, irritation, impatience, and disappointment. There is a danger especially of disappointment because the results will not seem to correspond to the investment of energy, and disappointment also to the extent that things which ought to be seen only as means—and as external means—are taken as ends having a value in themselves.

Also, the more one involves himself in liturgical renewal, with the questionings, the working hypotheses that it presupposes, the more one must remember that this renewal—as, in fact, all liturgy as a human technique—is relative. It is relative in the sense of not being absolute, of being secondary; it is even more relative in the sense of being "in relation" to something else, of deriving its meaning and all its value from a reality that will always infinitely surpass it.

Relative to what? Let the witness of three nuns answer that question. The following quotations are of particular interest because they are taken from personal letters written spontaneously, with no thought that they would be quoted or serve as witness. Note, also, that these three sisters cannot really be suspected of reacting against liturgical renewal, because at the time they were writing, each had received in her convent the responsibility of leading the liturgical *aggiornamento* because of her own desire for renewal. Liturgical action and its renewal are relative to the liturgy as the act of Christ. Grasping this will prevent us from projecting ourselves into the future to the point of bypassing that which is already given.

I wonder if our efforts at liturgical renewal would not gain depth if they were more centered on Christ, "the Lord of the liturgy" as the Eastern Christians say.

You see, I am persuaded that the evolution of liturgical forms is only in its beginning, and that all present reform must be placed under the sign of the "dynamic of the provisional" and of "unanimity in pluralism." But I also think that, as it presently exists and as imperfect as it remains, the liturgical celebration can be lived as the act of Christ and of the total Christ. Isn't the life of Christ in his Church—the very essence of which must be understood, shared, and expressed—somewhat put in the shade by the search for recipes for a better understanding, participation, expression, etc.? Whatever the form of our celebrations, are they not fraternal meetings around the resurrected Lord, who performs his passover in every baptized heart which is full of the Spirit?

It seems to me that we run the danger of forgetting what is essential and already present in the Church by expecting "something better." If we do not work for the renewal of the liturgy by living intensely our present liturgical life, our labor will be in vain—and outside the Lord.

Liturgy, then, in its human realization and its renewal, is relative to fraternal love, to the community, and to an unlimited love beyond the community.

> Yes, this work of liturgical renewal, like everything that I undertake, moreover, thrills me—calmly, but nothing that I *do* seems essential to my monastic vocation. That which we *become* under the action of the Spirit is what is essential, it seems to me. Therefore, our only mission, more urgent than ever, remains *love*.

> The other day I understood suddenly that I had taken a wrong direction in thinking it was good to try to improve the liturgy even to the point of being irritated by the obstacles. I said to myself, no, there is the liturgy of persons, that face-to-face celebration in the relationship of friendship. Drinking of the same cup creates ties which must be lived concretely, with loving concern, whatever happens. First, to *live* the liturgy, to flower on the bush where one is planted, with its blossoms and thorns and, in that experience, Christian charity constructs the liturgy and vice versa.

Moreover, critical and creative transformations of the liturgy are relative to the spiritual conversion of persons. If not, they can become an enterprise of unconscious self-justification, of affirming and seeking self, an escape into illusion:

> I have the impression that at least on the group level we have too much of a tendency to dissociate the

144

reexamination of liturgical and monastic questions from a clear look at our personal conversion, at the way in which we use the imperfect instruments that God has placed in our hands, at our loyalty in faithfulness. There is a risk of dissociation and an even greater danger that bringing things up to date dispenses with conversion. I experience it on my part.

Finally, liturgical changes are at the service of a prayer that liturgy itself is not able to express entirely. Both liturgy and contemplation are necessary. Sometimes we expect too much of the liturgy, as if it could express the totality and the diversity of our being before God. In doing so, we wrong the liturgy and are always disappointed by it; meanwhile we must question and examine ourselves about our contemplation.

Liturgical *aggiornamento* is an endless enterprise. I begin to be tired of it without having changed my ideas on the necessity of renewal. But I need very much to return to silent prayer.

Besides, experience has proven a hundred times that if I am not open to contemplation, I cannot truly be involved in the acts of the liturgy—in singing, in hearing the Word. I cannot become involved in it and I haven't much in me to involve . . . . I come to the "sharing of life," which is choral prayer, without having anything to share and without knowing how to share, for lack of having lived, very implicitly sometimes, my relationships with my sisters in the silent relation to God in contemplation.

And then it is especially in silent prayer that, as Karl Barth says, I sense myself as "definitively amazed." I understand that ancient monasticism made a great case for the gift of tears and of the

145

wringing of the heart, which is not an unpleasant sadness. God is always "too much." He is too far and too near. He loves us too much. He is too much ours, too much the heart of our heart, too vulnerable, too involved with what is human, too much put in question by our freedom. I understand that to contemplate him makes us weep, without our leaving that climate of simplicity and of confident joy which is our true death to ourselves. Let us permit him to act in us and to activate us.

Renewal Is Primarily Interior and Personal

In this connection, recall what I said earlier about the renewal of the language of prayer through meditation and contemplation, about the spiritual concern for recovering words in their depth and their transcendence, in their capacity to surprise and to express our intimate being. This should be our first reaction to and our constant vigilance in fighting against any formalism in the expressions and gestures of the liturgy. Is it not simply formalism in reverse to attack prayer only from the outside, to criticize the forms, as we are tempted to do today? This is a lazy solution, infantile and finally sterile. To what extent do we blame the forms of the liturgy to avoid asking if the emptiness is not within ourselves?

More than theology, more than preaching, more than witness, the liturgy is necessarily very closely bound not only to the themes but to the language of the Bible. If this were not so, the Bible would become at best an ancient reference document. It would no longer have a direct and living impact on the spirit of Christians. When preaching is too

146

much subjected to the vocabulary of Scripture, it merely repeats it; that is bad preaching, for it fails in its task of bringing the word of God to contemporary life. The essential function of liturgy, on the contrary, is not the up-dating of biblical language. Rather, its task is to keep us familiar with it. And this specifies and limits the possible changes of liturgical language.

Even if Bonhoeffer later expressed a more critical wish for a nonreligious language to speak of God, what he wrote about Christian vocabulary remains true of the liturgy:

> We are not able to remedy the fact that Christianity is two thousand years old and that it has its own language . . . . Everything depends on the depth and context from which our words issue . . . . You no doubt know the books of Bernanos? When the priests speak in them, their words carry weight. The reason for that is simply that they do not come from abstract reflection or stylistic observance, but very simply from the daily and personal dealing with Christ crucified. The terrible danger of spiritual small talk can be warded off only where the word flows, so to speak, directly from the cross of Jesus Christ, and where the Christ is so present that he speaks the words himself.[1]

There is a necessary reciprocity between intimate contemplation and the liturgy. "One upholds the other" (Rule of Taizé). Common prayer gives to contemplation an élan and a certain objectivity, guarding it from reducing itself too much to the limits of the individual. And contemplation protects the liturgy from being lived in a depersonalizing

147

objectivity. It is contemplation alone that can return to and ponder the words of the liturgy, that can slip within them, letting them resound in silence. It is contemplation that permits us to prepare to enter into the movement of the liturgy, that can prolong common prayer in order to grasp and interiorize that which verbal expression can only suggest of the mystery of God and of the mystery of our response.

The inadequacy of our language in speaking to God and about God does not mean that the choice of language doesn't matter. On the contrary, a demand for theological truth and spiritual beauty must preside over the formal renewal of that language. And the same need will make us discern that which remains irreplaceable in biblical and traditional language. But ancient or modern, the language of prayer will not escape immediate erosion and formalism unless silent contemplation transforms it into a language of love and wonder.

Spiritual reading is also important in keeping liturgical language alive and new. The reading of modern commentaries on Scripture leads us back to the original meaning of biblical terms by restoring their historical and religious context. Reading the early Church Fathers and the authors of the Middle Ages—all of them finally commentators on Scripture—renews our understanding of the symbolic and poetic nature of Christian language. In this resides the value of their typology and allegory, even when the latter seems a little strained to us. The reading of more recent or present-day authors helps us make the connection between the human sensibilities of our times and the culture of the prophets and apostles.

Balance between Novelty and Tradition

It is good that the liturgy must be celebrated daily and that nevertheless it pre-exists us. It is good that it mobilizes our initiative, and that at the same time we have to conform to it and let ourselves be carried by it. It is good that we express ourselves personally through the liturgy, while at the same time it takes us outside ourselves and makes us hear and say words that would not have come to our lips spontaneously at that moment. It is good that we draw the liturgy to ourselves to make it contemporary, while it draws us to itself to free us from our limitations and our shrunken little universe.

We approach this paradox from the angle of freedom. Freedom clearly seems to require the liturgy to include a margin of surprise and invention, room for the spontaneity of individuals, openings for the expression of themes suggested by current events. Freedom also seems to require a liturgy that evokes and integrates new forms: spontaneous creations such as meditations, for example, or prepared and elaborated creations such as hymns.

But is this the only form of freedom to be sought in the liturgy?

Experience shows, however, that no one is able to create with constant freshness. Spontaneous words are often dull, and their variety has limits that are not easy to broaden. If one seeks each day to choose the biblical elements of the service and to make up the prayers on the spur of the moment, there is a great risk of turning round and round within a thematically restricted horizon. Additionally, the spontaneity, the choices, and the invention that appeal to one person are not necessarily freedom for another; on the contrary, they may strike him as subservience.

Is the liturgy then—in what it contains of organization, appropriateness, and planning—a palliative unfortunately necessary because of the limits inherent in our spontaneity? That would be saying that, lacking the ability always to create something new, one should fall back on the old and traditional as better than nothing.

That is surrender to a very partial understanding of freedom, one reduced here to the limits of spontaneity. For if there is a freedom that invents, there is also one that assimilates. The former seizes the event in a spontaneous movement of welcome; the latter extracts from repetition the possibility of a mastery and a more profound search. The former flows out and exteriorizes; the latter digs deep and interiorizes.

Consequently, in their own way, length, repetition, and familiar and habitual surroundings can and must be agents of freedom: a freedom that avoids the ever-present threat of routine that some equate with habit. We should not confuse habit, which is a way of mastering oneself through a repeated exercise, with routine, which is the corruption of habit.

In no relatively serious area of life can one skimp on initiation or training, which requires repetition and perseverance and which increases emotional, intellectual, and physical control. Liturgy and prayer are no exception. The service will be impoverished if its elements, words, and symbolism must all be self-evident right from the start and justified by the present moment. On the contrary, it is good and necessary that a certain spiritual depth and some resonance of language should appear only after a time, through practice. It is good also that certain words and certain gestures of the liturgy should not have to change, because they witness to that which is not transitory, to that which never grows old.

A certain order is a condition of freedom, especially when several persons are involved. At the same time freedom has a special need to enter into the cyclic rhythm of things and of times—a rhythm that becomes part of our inner order and of the order that surrounds us. A Protestant deaconess said recently:

> In a common action, order and discipline are agents of peace and are the condition of true freedom. One of the characteristics of liturgical prayer is rhythm, which is produced by the regular repetition of a single element. It is one of the factors of beauty in art. All our life is woven with the most varied rhythms: day and night, seasons, inhaling and exhaling, hunger and fullness, etc. In the liturgy, repetition, which is found to be fatiguing by those who live it superficially, is rather a vital element. God deepens within us the place of his presence by the return each year of the same holy days, by the periodic repetition of the same readings, the same prayers. As it is necessary for us to have the same daily bread to subsist, so

it is necessary each day to say: Kyrie eleison and *Alleluia,* and we must also each day receive his Word, which is always the same and is always new.

So freedom does not lie only in the impromptu word or action; it lies also in the familiar action, tested by practice, or in the text that one knows by heart, that one has assimilated by repetition, that one can sing in chorus without difficulty in a dim light. In the same way, freedom lies not only in the possibility of choosing texts and putting together a service for some special occasion; it also lies in the lists of readings and in the plan of the established order of service, as a way to live, day by day, a prayer open to the totality of the revelation.

Freedom can, therefore, be found in the new and the unpublished or in the old and familiar. In either case it is not automatic. It requires that we want and are able to make our own the unpublished and the familiar, this novelty and that tradition.

We know how an established liturgical tradition erected into an absolute principle can lead into servitude. But perhaps we also know that we do not necessarily experience very satisfying freedom in an improvised and hesitant service. With hands full of mimeographed sheets, we find ourselves straining over a melody only half figured out and then glancing about wondering who knows what to do next.

After all, if in the liturgy, as in all human life, the new and the old are not mutually exclusive, it is because invention and assimilation, spontaneity and experience are two faces of our freedom—not opposed, but interrelated. There is the freedom that springs up suddenly and one that deepens from day to day. We must dig patiently so that the spontaneous is possible; we must also dig so that the spontaneous be received and become enriched, instead of being lost.

Ordinary Language and Liturgical Language

As everyone knows, there is a marked difference between liturgical language and the language used in everyday life, not only in vocabulary but, more profoundly, in intention. I propose to show here that this difference cannot be completely eliminated, and that to attempt to do so would be to the detriment of the liturgy. The difference must be accepted as a necessary tension, even if it is uncomfortable.

First, we must recognize the fact that ordinary language today is strongly influenced by the language of science and technology. That is an operational language whose words are strictly univocal, a precise language that voluntarily limits itself to a specific approach to reality. Modern science is based on a decision to forego the symbolic reading of the world, so that rational thought always tends to divest itself of language that is symbolic and, therefore, ambiguous.[2] This use of unambiguous language is intimately bound to the methodological decision, characteristic of the natural and social sciences, which prescinds from God, revelation, and all the supernatural dimensions of man and the universe. That decision, in so far as it is methodological, is wholly justified, if only by its results. But in the spirit of scientific and technological man and, more generally, in the civilization that is influenced by his science and technology, it runs a strong risk of passing unperceived from a particular methodological level to the general level considered to be intellectual evidence. In one stroke this strictly unambiguous language comes to appear the only serious approach to reality, and the reality that it apprehends is conceived as the whole of reality.

The language of the liturgy is symbolic from necessity; its meaning, what it designates, evokes another level of meaning that can be attained only in and through its first level of meaning. Additionally, liturgical language is symbolic because through it man understands and expresses himself as a being for whom reality (life, the world, others) is not primarily an object of scientific knowledge; it does not reduce itself to the objectivity of science but receives its meaning from its relationship to God.

Today, ordinary language—and the conception of the world that shapes it—is strongly marked by the scientific and technological approach. However, even one's body is a symbol, and our fundamental relationship to the world and to other persons cannot be expressed without recourse to symbolic language. This contradiction between two languages (one of which is more or less suppressed although it cannot be made to disappear) is one of the components of today's cultural malaise.

For many people today, the traditional language and gestures of the liturgy seem out of step with secular life and its language. But the opposite is also evident: secular life, with its restricted apprehension of reality, is itself often out of step with a whole

154

way of grasping and expressing existence, a way that is founded on and centered in God. This is not primarily a question of vocabulary; it is not even a specifically liturgical problem. More fundamentally it is the tension between two different approaches to reality: one, efficient and reductive; the other, whole and attentive to transcendence.

There is no question of suppressing this tension. Christians are especially sensitive to it, often to the point of embarrassment. But it exists, more or less hidden, in all men because they cannot be satisfied with being reduced to objects or with viewing the universe only as an object.

Certainly it is essential for the liturgy and its language to undergo a certain adaptation to the surrounding culture, in order to avoid freezing this tension into some sort of spiritual schizophrenia. But the movement to adapt the liturgy must be joined by an effort to open our secular life and everyday language to the vision of reality expressed in Scripture and the liturgy—the reality of man and world as essentially qualified by their relation to God.

Thus, two reciprocal adaptations are necessary. Presently it is the former, the liturgy, that is easier to accomplish and that is being urged upon us from all sides. But it is the second, the adaptation of our current secular life, that is more important and more difficult. We do not criticize the method that is basic to science and technology, rather we protest against a kind of imperialism in that method—an imperialism in itself not at all scientific. Then, perhaps, a more fortunate dialectic than exists today will be established between unambiguous and symbolic language. Meanwhile, we must put up with the tension courageously and without embarrassment, knowing that to affirm the legitimacy of the symbolic language of faith and of liturgy is one way to serve mankind. For all men —Christian or not—must understand themselves as transcendent subjects, irreducible to things.

The peculiarities of both of these languages must be safeguarded. Very legitimately, ordinary language—to the extent that it reflects a scientific vision of the world and of man—cannot become the language of liturgy without alteration. In the same way, science cannot be expected to renounce its methodology, which is based on deliberate disregard of God and all transcendence.

There is another reason why liturgy cannot use, unaltered, the language and gestures of ordinary life—a reason bound to the pejorative meaning that the adjective "ordinary" can have. Our life, our thought, our most contemporary words are constantly menaced by degradation and devaluation. As a result of our inclination to facile banality, they tend to lose their quality and density, to become superficial. Almost unavoidably, a laziness of spirit, a negligence of heart and of intelligence, a lack of attention let entire sectors of our existence and a large portion of the words and phrases of our speech fall into routine and insignificance.

It is important, therefore, for the liturgy to demand quality of language, to challenge banality and platitudes, to reject a slick facility of words, gestures, sounds, and rhythms. The liturgy cannot put

156

up with just any expressions, spoken any old way, nor can God's glory be celebrated with the music of taverns or with simple ditties. High standards will serve not only the honor of God, but that of mankind as well.

Here again is the dialectical tension between ordinary and liturgical language. It is legitimate to criticize and to adapt the liturgy in view of modern sensibility and expression. But change must not become simple conformity, for such adaptation calls in return for an opening of our entire daily lives to the purposes of the liturgy. We know very well that we do not enter into the liturgy without a profound and constantly renewed conversion of heart and mind. To encounter God in common worship is to put aside inner distraction and negligence, which corrupt and unravel all that they touch. To encounter God in the liturgy requires us to renounce the vulgarity that takes possession of all our emotions, our tastes, and our attitudes as soon as we place ourselves at the center and make ourselves the criterion of what is good and beautiful.

In the midst of an earthly life that always tends to exist only for itself, the liturgy, like prayer in general, recalls the truth and the necessity of consecration. Without being cut off from the secular, the liturgy does not need to be merely secular and ordinary. On the contrary, it should signify that, even at the center of secular life, there is nothing purely secular within a human and Christian existence that knows itself to come from God and wishes to be consecrated to God.

Recalling in this way the liturgical necessity for a

serious conversion of our minds in order to escape from inner vulgarity and negligence, recalling the aim of consecration that the liturgy must impress upon all of our daily lives—must not such recollection also be concerned with expressing the mentality and the language of daily life? Agreeing to cross a threshold to enter into the liturgy, and agreeing that its language is to be judged for its quality, its depth, and its possible transfiguration, must we not agree that that language must become more truly human in order to become at the same time worthy of God?

Secularize the liturgy? Yes, but with great discretion. For in ordinary life the liturgy must remain above the commonplace as a relief from platitudes, as an opening to the transcendent meaning of the everyday. As for the choice of language, the requirements of the liturgy will in the end serve a true secularization—one that is able to apprehend the world and man as they are truly constituted, in their autonomy. But for the Christian, this is possible only within a fundamental relationship to God, which specifically grants creation its own consistency and its relative autonomy. It is that relationship to God which is expressed in the liturgy, and it must be expressed in a particular way, according to its own rules, in a dialectical tension with everyday life. This is the best service that liturgy can render to the truth of secularization.

Feast Days and Everyday

It is not humanly possible to make every day a feast day. It is therefore legitimate that, in contrast to the liturgy of designated feast days, the liturgy of everyday should reflect, through its order and recurrence, the continuity and the humility of daily life. There is peace in such order and continuity. And that peace, which is a gift of God, is the structure which prepares for the feast day and the background against which the most eventful aspects of the liturgy stand out in relief. Repetition and creativity mutually protect each other from being fatiguing and disappointing.

But even if all days are not meant to be feast days, each day's liturgy must remain a celebration that moves beyond the ordinary, an opening of the everyday to the breakthrough of the Kingdom. This is why the liturgy cannot adopt just any language. The liturgy serves the everyday and the secular by remaining a bit alien; it deserves a spiritual and formal quality, a conversation of man and a transfiguration of his language.

NOTES

1. Dietrich Bonhoeffer, "Lettre à une inconnue" (Spring 1940?) *Textes choisis,* Le Centurion–Labor et Fides (Paris and Geneva 1970), pp. 318–319.

2. On this subject, see P. Colin, "Phenoménologie et herméneutique du symbole liturgique," in *La Liturgie après Vatican II,* Unam Sanctam 66 (Paris: La Cerf, 1967), pp. 214 ff.

6

The prayer of married couples

The prayer of married couples deserves some special attention.* In fact, in speaking with couples one comes to understand that the prayer of two married Christians is not simply a special case of common prayer. It constitutes a somewhat different spiritual phenomenon. Between two persons, especially two persons whose lives are intimately united, the agreement necessary in order for them to pray together is especially demanding. It is not easy to find a time during the day that is convenient for both of them. But the question of time often hides another question, that of establishing a spiritual communion that is great enough for common expression in prayer. The personal histories and sensibilities of the partners may be very diverse, and this diversity becomes even more marked when they pray as two rather than in a large assembly.

* In a slightly different form, these pages have appeared in *Foyers mixtes* 6 (January 1970) 8 ff.

It is usually thought that the spiritual accord necessary for prayer is more difficult to attain in a mixed marriage. This is far from certain. The mixed marriage (provided, of course, that it unites two practicing Christians who have decided to make their marriage a way of ecumenical unity) may even be advantageous: the partners are more conscious of the diversity, so that it may become for them a springboard instead of an obstacle. They also have the advantage of being better able to discern, from the beginning, that their diversity must not only be taken seriously but must be respected as a possible enrichment.

A Preliminary Conviction

Speaking from experience, many couples who possess the desire for conjugal prayer testify that it is certainly difficult to persevere in that prayer. But the greatest difficulty is that of daring to begin or to start over after an interruption—of surmounting the impression of artificiality—and the longer one waits the more difficult it becomes.

Since that difficulty seems to be so great, it is necessary to pose a basic question: *why* does a couple want to pray together, why do they persist?

One generally asks, when beginning something, *how* to go about it? And, in fact, the difficulty of conjugal prayer necessitates concrete preparations, a certain know-how, and decisions that both partners try to hold to.

However, the more the question *how* is posed with

discernment and is found to be important, the more the question *why* must be put first. It is necessary to know for what cause one wishes to work. If not, the efforts and decisions will give the married couple the feeling of legal obligations, of constraint that crushes them, and may very soon make them feel disgusted with prayer or, at least, increase the feeling of artificiality. On the other hand, if the conviction with which decisions have been made is very strong, the will to cleave to these decisions and the efforts to carry them out can be correspondingly great. But what conviction? That of the special meaning of conjugal prayer, of its cogency, and of the correctness of its very principle.

Why should a married couple pray together? Because it is good? Because they ought to do so? Because they feel the desire or the need? These are insufficient answers, unless it is specified that this good, this rightness, this desire or need relates to what is most essential for that marriage and that it springs logically from the couple's Christian faith.

There is an answer however, which, in the logic of faith, tries to express the essential reason. Grace is not a thing, but a gesture of God on our behalf, a sign of his presence in our lives. So we can receive this grace only by relating it to God in a movement of recognition and gratitude, by responding to the friendship of God with a movement of friendship—of which prayer is a major and necessary expression. If it is good, just, and logical that marriage partners undertake prayer together as well as separately, is it not because ultimately their conjugal love itself appears to them as a grace from

163

God? It is a grace because, as on the first day of their engagement and on their wedding day, each discerns, by faith, a gift and a presence of Christ in the person of the other and in the life that they build in common. This conjugal grace, in order to be received and to remain alive, requires expression in a conjugal prayer that acknowledges that grace before God in thanksgiving (it being understood that thanksgiving involves all forms of prayer).

It is given to Christian married couples to hear and to receive very concretely, through their love and unity, this promise of the Lord: "Blessed are those who are invited to the marriage supper of the Lamb" (Rev. 19:9). It is, therefore, right and just, if a couple are truly to receive that promise and to make their common life a parable of the love of God, that they be united in a prayer that might be summed up: "Yes, Lord, we are happy to be your guests and, in the conjugal unity you have given us, to live the nuptial parable of your eternal Kingdom."

A Sudden Timidity

If we are convinced of the meaning of conjugal prayer, then we can approach the question of how a couple is to pray. Many couples find that they experience what they call a sudden timidity when they attempt to pray together. "To pray together in a group, or even with children, is easy; when it is just the two of us, something seems to block it," married couples report.

The difficulty may often exist on the very concrete level of the *expression* of prayer. In fact, it seems that many couples do not see their prayer as a kind of community prayer, but as the same kind of prayer one undertakes when one is alone with God. But characteristically such prayer is not expressed in carefully constructed phrases or in relatively logical trains of thought. It remains largely incommunicable, not necessarily in its content but in its form.

Thus, when the two partners wish to transpose this very personal prayer into words and sentences, they often find themselves embarrassed. They are embarrassed by a feeling of artificiality, by a feeling of having to give a speech while someone else listens, by the difficulty of entering into another person's formulation. Pastoral counseling provides evidence that this problem, which, on the surface, seems unimportant and which is generally unconscious, is, in fact, very significant for many couples.

Perhaps it would be more realistic to recognize that the prayer of married couples is a special type of community prayer. Such prayers necessarily require a certain objectivity of expression, so that they can express each person fairly well, although not perfectly. But a couple can also legitimately perceive that the communion that characterizes their relationship—and the prayer that expresses it—is also far more intimate than any other form of community. Furthermore, their prayers may seem artificial if they are solely and extremely objective.

Must we conclude, therefore, that the partners either must have identical ways of expressing themselves in intimate and personal prayer (which would be rare and improbable) or must renounce efforts to pray together? No, for one can pray with another person without necessarily saying the entire prayer aloud. Some couples have found their method to be simply agreeing on the themes for their prayer, saying "let us pray for . . . ," and then naming the children, relatives, friends, the life of the Church and of the world, and so on. Such a form of prayer is naturally objective and does not appear either artificial or intimidating. And it allows for silence in which both partners can express the prayer in innermost hearts.

Thus the obstacle of "timidity" can be overcome if the married couple's prayer expresses, without precise formulation, their most intimate and personal concerns. But it is also important that this prayer, in order not to dry up, be founded upon the couple's reading Scripture together, and that it acquire an objective dimension from certain psalms and readings from Christian liturgy. Finally, one must remember, not as an imposed rule but as a fact of experience, that even conjugal prayer in its special intimacy cannot replace the personal prayer of each partner to God. All human communion, in order to be true, remains a unity of two persons, each of whom is unique in the eyes of God. This is why there must be a reciprocity between the individual prayer of each partner and their prayer together.

A Decision that Anticipates Exceptions

Many couples come to recognize that their prayer will soon become rare or nonexistent if dependent on chance circumstances or spontaneous and simultaneous mutual wish. In the logic of faith, they resolve, therefore, that their prayer will be regular and will not depend upon the mood of the moment. Regular may mean weekly, or even daily, but it must mean at a fixed interval and it implies also the minimal organization that such regularity requires.

Psychological and spiritual obstacles begin to fade away when a joint decision is made to pray regularly, instead of waiting for the mood of prayer to descend simultaneously on both partners. It seems that the wise audacity of such a decision must be accompanied by another wisdom, that of accepting as inevitable the interruptions that occasionally arise against one's will and not seeing these interruptions as a reversal of the decision to pray. For to interpret these as failures would paralyze the decision to pray and soon lead to its abandonment.

Reversing Roles

It is almost inevitable that one of the two partners will take greater care to remember and keep alive the regularity of prayer. But in the long run this situation can become a burden. It may place both partners in artificial roles from which they cannot escape. Being constantly exhorted puts one on the defensive. To be constantly exhorting in the end paralyzes initiative or makes one aggressive. To seem more pious or less pious may induce subjective feelings of guilt or a mutual sitting-in-judgment that lacks objective basis. For this reason, husband and wife must be able from time to time to discuss this psychological phenomenon with each other and, if possible, to agree to take turns in initiating prayer. The most important thing, however, is to remember often and together that the decision has been made and carried out by common agreement, for that on this condition it remains free, viable, and joyous.